"Analyn and Brandon Miller have created one of the best places to start developing a parenting approach based in strengths!"
Tom Rath, researcher and author of the *New York Times* number one bestseller *StrengthsFinder 2.0*

"This book is a powerful and empowering read for any parent who wants to bring out the God-given gifts in their child."
Lea Waters, psychologist and author of *The Strength Switch: How the New Science of Strength-Based Parenting Can Help Your Child and Your Teen to Flourish*

"*Play to Their Strengths* will help you become a better parent and your child become the best they can be."
Dave Ferguson, pastor and author of *Hero Maker: 5 Essential Practices for Leaders to Multiply Leaders*

"In *Play to Their Strengths,* Brandon and Analyn Miller lay out a clear and easily adaptable path for seeing each child as a unique individual, ready to give the world the contribution they were brought into this life to give."
Jenifer Fox, author of *Your Child's Strengths*

"Real, practical, and very helpful."
Greg Haswell, pastor and author of *Beyond Leadership*

"This book is a must-read for parents who want to help their children grow their strengths!"
Victor Seet, founder of StrengthsSchool™ and the first Gold Gallup-Certified StrengthsFinder® Coach

"In this age of parenting the perfect child and the stress that goal brings, this tremendously powerful resource offers a quieter, stronger, more effective approach."
Maureen Electa Monte, author of *Destination Unstoppable: The Journey of No Teammate Left Behind*

"Full of divine wisdom, inspiration, and practical frameworks, this book educates, inspires, and guides you to your best self in parenting."
Taisja Laudy, founder of TL&C Global

"The Millers have skillfully combined their strong faith, their love of family, and their belief in strengths to create a powerful how-to book for parents who want to bring out the best in their kids and themselves."

Sara Robinson, author of
Unstuck at Last: Using Your Strengths to Get What You Want

"This book cuts through parenting myths that burden and confuse us and shows practical ways to nurture our children's natural gifts and talents."

Sara Regan, CEO of Strengths Now and author
of *Strengths Boost: Partnering for Success*

"The methods and strategies in this amazing book are timely and relevant for any generation and any family."

Rhonda Knight Boyle, coauthor of *Turning Talents into Strengths: Stories of Coaching Transformation*

"While reading *Play to Their Strengths*, all I could think about was how fast I wanted to give a copy to my son and daughter-in-law as new parents of my first grandchild."

Brent O'Bannon, author of *Let's Talk Strengths*

"This book is a game changer!"

Nicole Seichter, author of *Enjoy: A New Approach to Stress and Burnout Prevention*

"Every parent who is serious about raising children to be who God made them to be ought to read this book!"

Chris Heinz, author of *Made to Pray*

"Read this book, share it with your spouse, celebrate it with your children, and change your family."

Paul Porter, StrengthsFinder® consultant
and former school superintendent

"A practical and inspiring guide for families."

Lisa Cummings, founder of *Lead Through Strengths*

"*Play to Their Strengths* gives parents a paradigm shift in their thinking, allowing them to see their children the way God intended—as amazing gifts with God-given talents and strengths that make them uniquely special."
Ryan and Jennifer Miller, family and marriage ministry

"This book introduces an approach to parenting that is guaranteed to increase the love and reduce the stress and conflict in our homes."
Ryan Darby, PhD

"A refreshing and inspiring companion on your parenting journey."
Kathy Kerston, Gallup-Certified StrengthsFinder® Coach

"Asking your kids, 'What's *strong* with you?' instead of asking, 'What's *wrong* with you?' is a huge shift in parenting that the Millers invite parents to consider."
Sandie Haskins, pastor and International Coaching Federation coach

"*Play to Their Strengths* is chock-full of tactical, relatable, and tangible steps that parents in any season of parenting can start implementing immediately for real, sustainable impact on that sacred relationship."
Darren Virassammy, COO and cofounder of 34 Strong, Inc.

"A refreshing lens for affirming, honoring, and empowering the best in children."
Adriane Massey, founder and president of Strengths Zone

"There is a better way to raise our children! *Play to Their Strengths* is such a powerful book for all parents, grandparents, and caregivers."
Murray Guest, CEO of Inspire My Business

"I loved every single page of this book and experienced more than a handful of powerful mindset-changing moments that have already affected the relationship with my kids."
Peter Baloh, partner and senior consultant of e2grow

PLAY TO THEIR STRENGTHS

ANALYN & BRANDON
MILLER

HARVEST HOUSE PUBLISHERS
EUGENE, OREGON

Cover design by Bryce Williamson

Cover photos © -VICTOR-, Fedora Bradas, sirup, ExpressIPhoto / Getty Images

Play to Their Strengths
Copyright © 2019 by Brandon Miller and Analyn Miller
Published by Harvest House Publishers
Eugene, Oregon 97408
www.harvesthousepublishers.com

ISBN 978-0-7369-7617-6 pbk.
ISBN 978-0-7369-7618-3 eBook

Library of Congress Cataloging-in-Publication Data

Names: Miller, Brandon, author. | Miller, Analyn, author.
Title: Play to their strengths / Brandon and Analyn Miller.
Description: Eugene, Oregon : Harvest House Publishers, [2019] | Includes
   bibliographical references.
Identifiers: LCCN 2018060615 (print) | LCCN 2019002431 (ebook) | ISBN
   9780736976183 (ebook) | ISBN 9780736976176 (pbk.)
Subjects: LCSH: Parenting—Religious aspects—Christianity. | Parent and
   child—Religious aspects—Christianity.
Classification: LCC BV4529 (ebook) | LCC BV4529 .M546 2019 (print) | DDC
   248.8/45—dc23
LC record available at https://lccn.loc.gov/2018060615

Printed in the United States of America

19 20 21 22 23 24 25 26 27 / VP-SK / 10 9 8 7 6 5 4 3 2 1

To our parents

Thank you for supporting us through our parenting journey and being continual sources of love and encouragement. It truly takes a community to raise children, and you have stood in the place of caregivers, truth bringers, and family builders.

We hope this book honors the legacy you have established.

Acknowledgments

To our children—thank you all for allowing us to love you, learn with you, and lead you. This book is your story, and the story goes on.

To the wonderful people at Harvest House—thank you for walking with us through this process. Your team has been amazing to work with!

To the teams at 34 Strong and Analyn Miller Group—thank you for your unwavering support and the continual encouragement you were to us as we made time to complete this work.

To our dear friend Jennifer—thank you for your part in helping us launch this project. We appreciate you.

To Ryan and Jen—thank you for the hours you spent with us helping to craft the Playbook. We love you both and appreciate you for lending us your experience and expertise.

To the legacy of Dr. Donald O. Clifton—we stand on the shoulders of his work with strengths and the continual efforts of his family through the Gallup organization.

To the members of the global strengths community—thank you all for the work you do and for your amazing support as we sought your feedback for the content of this work.

To our faith communities at Northlands Church, The Core Youth Movement, and Reflect Church—we feel your prayers, appreciate your love and support, and rejoice with you at the good work the Lord has done!

To the very best of friends, Thomas and Michele—your encouragement and support inspire us to keep reaching for all that God has for us. We love you both very much!

Contents

• • •

Foreword

Only a handful of experiences in life become more vivid with time. For me, this wonderful new book by Brandon and Analyn Miller, *Play to Their Strengths*, is a story so remarkable, it's become my go-to story whenever I've come face to face with a couple or family in need. I've drawn on this miracle family and their miracle story more times than I can remember, and every time it's provided profound hope in times of confusion and despair.

I first met Brandon and Analyn nearly 30 years ago while pastoring a small start-up church in Elk Grove, California. Life and church were simple back then. No social media, no internet, and no pressure to outperform another church. I miss those days.

Right in the middle of that simplicity, our young church experienced a moment of real testing. Two high school kids found themselves facing a future they never saw coming. I remember well the emotions and fears of that moment. For our young church family, we too were faced with a choice. Would we be religious or real? Was grace a theology or a practice? Looking back, Brandon and Analyn were a gift to me as a young pastor. I grew as they grew. I was discovering new levels of grace right alongside them. Now, years later, we see the full outcome of that grace. A beautiful baby girl has become a beautiful woman of

God. And those two frightened high school kids who chose to trust Christ through those fears have emerged as a voice to their generation.

Yes, grace did all of that.

Marriage is no ordinary promise. Brandon and Analyn Miller believe that deeply, and now God is rewarding them with no ordinary life. *Play to Their Strengths* is a fresh and dynamic game plan for young families. It gives parents a life-giving how-to for building their own family legacy. This book, born out of their own transformed and remodeled life, is a must for any family who is seeking excellence.

It was an honor to play a small part when this story began many years ago. I'm even more excited to see how God will multiply and use this story to help thousands of families in the future.

Scott Hagan
President, North Central University
Minneapolis, Minnesota

1

Inspire Your Kids to Shine

Affirming words from moms and dads are like light switches.
Speak a word of affirmation at the right moment in a child's
life and it's like lighting up a whole roomful of possibilities.

GARY SMALLEY

You are a parent who is invested in your kids. Chances are, you opened this book with the singular hope of being a better parent... the best parent you can be. We have this goal in common with you. In fact, for years we strove to be better and do better. Maybe you have done the same—maybe you are doing the same.

Then during one season of our family's journey, we found an uncommon way to truly be better parents. It changed everything. We can't wait to share with you this simple, intentional shift that will usher in life to your family and purpose to your child's path.

First, let's get a clear look at our "before" family picture.

From the moment we nervously brought home our first tiny bundle of huge responsibility, our focus was on our parenting and whether we were succeeding or failing in what is possibly the most important role in a person's life. Even if we didn't articulate it then, our governing question was, What should we do and what shouldn't we do as parents? It didn't occur to us to instead ask, Who is this child, and how do we parent her to become the person God made her to be?

As our family expanded, we noticed obvious differences among our kids, especially who slept through the night and who made bedtime feel like a circus without a ringleader. But when it came to daily living, priorities, and choices, we often unknowingly worked against their individual strengths as we nudged them to struggle forward in our strengths.

After years of missteps and frustrations and shaking our heads when a seemingly smart parenting practice didn't work yet again, we took stock. Let's face it, we were desperate.

We had a problem—and it wasn't our kids.

Little did we know that the answer was right in front of us—and it *was* our kids.

The singular focus of successful parenting isn't about being a perfect parent; it's about becoming a parent who notices and nurtures the best in a child.

We're here to share how this parenting perspective can inspire and transform your family. We know firsthand! This eye-opening approach will help you see your children for who they are and who they are meant to become so they can thrive in their destinies rather than unravel in mediocrity and confusion.

> The singular focus of successful parenting isn't about being a perfect parent; it's about becoming a parent who notices and nurtures the best in a child.

Will You Invest in the Myth or the Mission?

We married young and had three children by the age of 22. As young parents, we followed a traditional, hierarchal leadership approach to parenting. Though we loved our trio deeply and doted on them with nice stuff and great opportunities, we in fact missed the mark. We trusted the myth that our children existed to make us look good or feel good about how we parented. Our short-term goal was for the kids to always conduct themselves in the way we felt was appropriate, which would lead to our long-term goal of shaping our kids to become people we could be proud of because they represented us well and represented our version of success. We were more focused on creating replicas of what we thought a Miller child should be than on raising uniquely wired and talented children who would forge their own paths.

Sadly, we were muting our children's unique brilliance and our own personal strengths by parenting in a top-down, dictatorial style of leadership.

It wasn't until our first three children entered their teenage years that our parenting model floundered and was revealed as a myth instead of a mission. There was a disconnect between our ideals and the kids' individual interests and natural strengths. Pressures

> *"The strengths-based view gave my mom and dad a tool to better understand my siblings and myself and to teach life lessons in a way we would receive more readily."*
>
> **–LANCE (24)**

were mounting to be a certain way and to meet familial, societal, religious, and academic expectations that didn't necessarily fit with each of our children's hardwiring. Our aha moment came during an encounter between Brandon and our oldest son, Lance.

It was a hot August day in Sacramento, California, and I (Brandon) was driving Lance to his first day of football practice. Lance was joining the freshman football team at our local high school, and I had volunteered to serve as an assistant coach. As we drove, I was compelled to inspire him for greatness. I had rather successfully played the sport and spent some years coaching. I felt as though I could be a guide to my son—in essence, an expert to help him become his very best. I passionately told Lance how he would play with excellence and help his team as he exhibited eagerness and demonstrated his vital role on the squad.

Midspeech, Lance leaned over and put his hand on my shoulder, saying, "Dad, I just need you to know, I'm not like you, and I'm not going to play football the same way you did."

In a moment of shock, I found myself at a loss for words—a rarity, as anyone who knows me can attest. I looked over at him and grunted something along the lines of "Go get 'em, son" while pulling into the parking lot. That very ordinary moment started a shift in my thinking.

---

*We were more focused on creating replicas
of what we thought a Miller child should be
than on raising uniquely wired and talented
children who would forge their own paths.*

True to his word, Lance did not play football the way I did—he played his own way. He enjoyed being on the team his freshman year, but after the season ended, Lance hung up his jersey and pads and moved on to other things.

I realized I had to let go of who I thought Lance could be and how *my* identity and experience were supposed to help him get there. I needed to recalibrate and focus on my child's unique talents and wiring to coach him toward his version of success. I needed to let go of the myth and embrace the mission of nurturing this child's best by playing to his strengths.

A New Model for Parenting

During the summer after his freshman year, we more intentionally examined Lance's strengths. Unlike me, Lance is hardwired to enjoy working with his hands and creating or inventing new ways to get things done. As a kid, he tore apart his toys to make something new. We often found Lance with some kind of new invention. Remote-control cars would be taken apart and reconfigured with other toy parts to become motorized boats. To him, taking toys apart was as much fun as putting them together.

As Lance got older, this natural inclination led him to try a variety of sports, woodshop, academic endeavors, theater, and even auto mechanics. Lance had a lot of interests and was pretty good at most of what he tried. As his parents, we wondered how to develop a kid like that!

A strengths-based approach became imperative in our parenting journey, freeing us to focus on our son's intrinsic talent amid his ever-changing interests and activities. It took us a decade or so, but we realized how such awareness is pivotal to the development and outcome of our children's lives.

Watch for Shining Eyes

We watched Bailee, our oldest, struggle to find her place. She was shy, and we often watched her face situations with downcast eyes. But then one day, she stepped onto a stage during a drama class and her eyes lit up. We immediately noticed and helped cultivate this interest. Together, we discovered what made her shine with purpose and passion. The trajectory of Bailee's life shifted that year.

Our way to gauge strength and success in our children also shifted. We no longer count the number of As on report cards or medals won in sports to measure how we're doing or how our kids are doing. We watch our children to see when and how their eyes light up with joy and purpose. When Bailee stepped onto the stage, we saw a change—a spark that transformed her whole presence. That moment when her eyes were shining told us how our dear Bailee was going to do more than just survive adolescence.

As we supported her participation in a performing arts academy, we watched her insecurity fade and her confidence grow. New possibilities opened up, and her impact reached further than we ever imagined. We have seen that creating space for children to experience, discover, and apply their unique talents allows them to find their versions of success and fulfillment.

Creating space for children to experience, discover, and apply their unique talents allows them to find their versions of success and fulfillment.

This idea of looking for shining eyes as an indicator of success comes from Benjamin Zander, world-renowned conductor of the Boston Philharmonic Orchestra. In his popular TED Talk of 2008, he said, "I have a definition of success. For me, it's very simple. It's not about wealth and fame and power. It's about how many shining eyes I have around me."[1] Zander realized the high cost of a top-down, hierarchal leadership style is the loss of engagement and self-expression among those being led. His epiphany was that as a conductor—with all his expertise—he doesn't produce a sound. The success of the orchestra comes from the interplay of sounds made by each member playing their own instruments brilliantly. Zander suddenly saw his role in a new light, understanding that his objective as the primary influencer was to bring out the unique talent in each player.

This revelation compelled Zander to rethink his role: "My job is to awaken possibility in other people. If their eyes are shining, you know you're doing it. If they're not shining, you get to ask the question, Who am I being that my players' eyes are not shining?"[2] This refreshing form of leadership takes us out of a paradigm defined by competition, fear, and pressure. Zander invites leaders to engage followers differently with the objective of drawing out and developing the unique talents of each follower. He learned he could determine his level of success by looking into the eyes of his followers. Shining eyes reflect individual brilliance, high engagement, and strong well-being.

Isn't this our hope for our children?

As parents, we serve as the most influential leaders throughout our children's development. We can apply Zander's question to our parenting journey: Who am I being that my children's eyes are not shining? Every step of this journey will encourage you to embrace parenting that develops the unique strengths of your children and creates shining eyes, alive to the passion and purposes they are meant to live out.

As parents, we serve as the most influential leaders throughout our children's early development.

God Crafted Our Kids

Parents have the unique opportunity to give their children eyes that shine by helping them connect their talents with opportunities at home, school, church, and beyond. Parents' mission is to propel their children into God's calling for their lives by nurturing their unique strengths. When we realized this, we became students of our children, focused on discovering their talents and watching for moments when their eyes lit up and their engagement level soared.

This shift has brought a new level of freedom into our home. Our kids feel less pressure, and they don't feel like we're comparing them to anyone. We experience the joy of walking with each of our kids down the path toward who God plans for them to become.

Our mission is to propel our children into God's calling for their lives by nurturing their unique strengths.

Scripture reveals that God "created mankind in his own image" (Genesis 1:27). Every human being is an image bearer of our Father in heaven, so aspects of each person's intrinsic nature reflect the nature of God himself. In our home, all our ideas about parenting rest on the core belief that God imbues each person with gifts that reflect his divine nature, such as compassion, creativity, or leadership. God made each child with a destiny, just as he did the prophet Jeremiah: "Before I formed you in the womb I knew you, before you were born I set you apart" (1:5). God has a great plan for children to shine brilliantly in their own unique way, demonstrating his goodness to the world around us. We initially failed to recognize the seeds of strength in our own first three little ones—Bailee, Lance, and Ciera—but God knew about them from the very beginning. He crafted their passions, personalities, and talents for their callings.

Developing children for a successful future is more about discovering their identities than adhering perfectly to a one-size-fits-all parenting strategy. If children are uniquely crafted by God, then reason demands that parents must guide each child uniquely according to that child's qualities.

From Our Family to Yours

We have been married for more than 25 years and are parents to four daughters and three sons. Their ages span 17 years. There are no his and hers in our family. Sometimes when people find out we have so many children, they ask if we are Mormon or Catholic or perhaps a blended family. We smile and respond, "Nope...we just played to our strengths and are blessed with a large, very dynamic family."

Our inspiration and motivation come from this rare experience of parenting a family of kids who span nearly a full generation. We have walked through each stage of raising a child multiple times! Each step of the way, we've learned more about the power of a strengths-based focus to lead each child in the way *he or she* should go. Throughout the book, we've sprinkled quotes from our Miller tribe.

Our three older kids are Bailee (25), Lance (24), and Ciera (22), and they all flew the coop. Bailee married Jordan (27); Lance married Christine (24), who gave birth to our first grandson, Harold (1); and Ciera married Adam (23). We have four kids still at home: Michaela (15), Madeline (14), David (12), and Daniel (9).

Back row: Michaela, Adam, Jordan, Lance
Middle Row: Madeline, Ciera, Bailee, Christine
Front Row: David, Brandon (Harold), Analyn, Daniel

Analyn works full-time as a successful real estate agent in the greater Sacramento area. She skillfully coordinates our children's engagements with business and community demands to create an intentional culture in our home valuing fun, relationships, and excellence. Our family has always valued the local church, and together we have served children, youth, and young adults in various ministry capacities for more than 20 years. Brandon is a Gallup Certified Strengths Coach and the CEO of 34 Strong, a coaching and consulting firm whose purpose is to build great places to work by shifting to a strengths-based developmental strategy.

We often find ourselves telling stories about our kids from the stage at workshops and seminars, among friends, and with coworkers in office lunchrooms. Parents of kids of every age want to know how we made the change to strengths-based parenting. They long to move beyond parenting myths and toward a higher mission.

When parents focus their energy on identifying their children's unique talents and help them move with their natural momentum toward their best possible outcomes, these mothers and fathers watch their children's downcast eyes become eyes that shine and look ahead with promise and engagement.

We team up along this journey to share our combined stories and insights on parenting to our kids' strengths. We don't claim to be parenting experts, but we offer our anecdotes as object lessons with the hope of illustrating the beauty and impact of an intentional parenting strategy that focuses on what's right with our kids rather than what's wrong.

Together, we've worked to incorporate the insights and object lessons that our unique family structure can humbly offer for the benefit of a wide range of families.

Your Journey, Your Playbook

If you're just beginning your parenting journey, we hope this book provides valuable insights that will empower you to start well. Maybe you are a little further down the path and will identify with the anecdotes and wisdom related to children, adolescents, and teens. If you are parenting young adults, we trust some of the lessons we share will provide helpful takeaways for you as well. The last two chapters of this book are dedicated to age-relevant information. We encourage you to read both chapters regardless of your child's age. You'll receive insight into your relationship with your child and what his or her needs are and will be along the way.

If you are parents through adoption, we hope this book will provide valuable insights as you raise your child in their forever family. And if you are caring for kids through foster care, we trust this book will give you direction as you share your love and home with those entrusted to your care.

Whatever season of parenting (or grandparenting) you are in, this journey of discovery is a personal one for you, and it's worth recording and discussing. So along the way, we'll encourage you to journal and to have meaningful conversations with your family. That's why we created the interactive Parenting Playbook at the end of the book. This is a chapter-by-chapter gathering of…

- practical steps and encouragements
- lists and charts to clarify and retain what you discover
- activities to do with your child and family to identify strengths
- discovery questions that will help you record your observations

Our hope is that this guide brings the message of every chapter to life—your life—to help you play to your child's strengths and embark on this transformative way to parent the child God has called you to grow. It can be used as either a personal parenting tool or a resource for small groups and classrooms. Also, at the end of each chapter, we've placed "Review the Play" questions to help you process the material and reveal simple takeaways to build on.

We believe great benefit and blessing can be found at any stage when you parent to a child's strengths. If pressure, comparison, and self-doubt are creeping into your parenting approach, be encouraged— we have been there! Now is the perfect time to trade in that frustration for a fresh fascination with your children.

—————————— **REVIEW THE PLAY** ——————————

1. What have you learned about yourself as a parent from this chapter's exploration?

2. What is one way this chapter helped you make a shift toward playing to your child's God-given strengths?

3. What did you discover about your child this week that surprises you or changes the way you interact with them?

4. Which insight or activity from this chapter's Playbook offering is the most helpful to your family right now? Why?

Check out the activities for chapter 1 in the Parenting Playbook on page 169.

2

Exchange Frustration for Fascination

Every baby born into the world is a finer one than the last.

CHARLES DICKENS

We will never forget our son Lance's excitement at his first baby's gender reveal party. Thirty family members gathered at Nana and Papa's house and watched as Lance's eyes shone like the sun when a special reveal cake indicated he was going to be a daddy to a son. He remained amazed and fascinated throughout the pregnancy and delivery…and has been awestruck every day since. He and his wife, Christine, are enthralled by their child's every movement, sound, expression, delight, and interest.

Seeing Lance and Christine's delight in Harold reminded us how special this stage of fascination is for most new parents. From the moment they find out they are pregnant or sign adoption papers, they begin to plan delivery or arrival-day strategies. They are full of curiosity and anticipation. Each glimpse of the baby in an ultrasound or photo is followed by countless conversations about what their child might be like.

Then the big day arrives when they get to hold their baby. Their perspective of their child in this moment is probably as pure as it will ever be. They see an absolute blessing, love personified, the fulfillment of dreams, and a bright future for this perfect bundle of joy. They watch one of their greatest dreams come to life, and their eyes (though often tired) are shining like they never have before. They know they will move heaven and earth to keep their child safe, make them happy, and see them thrive.

Parents are enthralled by the unique and even quirky characteristics their baby displays. The child can do no wrong, and the parents are his or her biggest fans. They are unequivocally fascinated with their baby. With new parents' pure perspective, they see only the good in this tiny human being, and they proudly tell everyone, in person and on social media, how charming and special their child is.

> **fascination** (*noun*): the state of being attracted to and held attentively by a unique power, personal charm, unusual nature, or some other special quality

When Fascination Fades

Parenting a baby for the first 12 months is all about discovery. What does she like? What puts him to sleep? What toys distract her? What kind of foods does he prefer? Parents become students as they learn how to feed their unique babies, put them to sleep, and engage them. But as little ones develop and start fighting nap time, throwing tantrums in the grocery store, and snatching toys from playmates, parents start employing every tactic they can think of to modify and guide their children's behavior.

The years that follow are laden with more decisions: stay at home or take the child to day care, spank or assign time-outs, break up fights or let them work it out, use natural oils or medications, enroll in public or private education, sign up for soccer or piano lessons...and the list just grows from there with increasing intensity and higher stakes. Add in their child's unique hardwiring and preferences, and suddenly they are welcoming a new companion into the home—frustration.

Parents' curiosity about their children can be dimmed by irritation from "toddlerisms." Tantrums, tears, and defiant wills leave parents exhausted and struggling to figure out how to mold children into the people they want them to be. Doting parents suddenly discover their precious babies have become willful toddlers. They know toddlers will assert themselves as they learn how to engage with the world around them, but most parents are still shocked to see the corresponding behavior. At this point, when new parents' shining eyes start to dull a bit, behavior becomes the new measuring stick for success—for both the child and the parents.

This shift from being fascinated by babies to traumatized by toddlers can set a negative course for a parenting strategy. Parents' love for their kids doesn't diminish, but the frustration of decision-making and behavioral training can cast a shadow over the child's formative years. Suddenly the adorable, helpful four-year-old begins telling lies. The sweet, funny little girl starts sassing and smacking. The focused, Lego-building toddler can't seem to get with the program and get out of the door for school. If it's not one thing, it's another.

As parents juggle so many needs and priorities, eventually their greatest desire can be for their child to exhibit uniform behavior and attitudes. Strong-willed children complicate everything, right? So parents strategize about how to get their kids to do what they want, experimenting with various kinds of positive reinforcement or the newest discipline tactic.

Suddenly they are focused only on what their child is doing wrong and how they can steer, coerce, or bribe the child toward change. What happened to the fascination?

We can tell you what happened in our home. We started to follow a parenting model we knew from our own families and from watching others around us. We were a family of faith, and yet grace and building up one another in our strengths were not our objectives. We wanted our kids to toe the line, follow instructions, and be who we wanted them to be. When we had a bad day, our attitude and perspective toward our kids were colored by our mood, and we would look for something wrong in their behavior.

We thought we had to be a certain way as parents, and we thought our children had to be a certain way too. Our shift wasn't just from fascination to frustration—it was also from fascination to fear. Fear of what? Pick your poison. We were afraid of not being good parents, of failing our kids, of not "getting it right." We worried about whether we were choosing the right schools, diets, doctors, and extracurricular activities. And to be completely honest, we worried we would look bad or our kids would reflect badly on us. This cycle of fear only sent us further into frustration.

Unfortunately, for most parents, the knee-jerk reaction to frustration is wielding behavior modification as a tool to make children act right and be better. Behavior modification produces long-term success only if the parents maintain the standard perfectly. But of course, perfection is impossible, so behavior modification inevitably leads to failure, producing shame in children and parents alike. This is not what we are after, but it is the pit parents easily fall into because raising kids is hard. Feeling frustrated at times is natural for parents, but when the atmosphere at home is defined by frustration, that's a red flag.

The Red Flag of Frustration

For a season, frustration became a thief in the Miller home, stealing our delight in and discovery of each of our children. With multiple kids screaming and running in different directions, we found ourselves yelling constantly, punishing harshly, and regularly asserting our authority and their inferiority. We were constantly irritated, and they were constantly pushing back against our control.

For a season, frustration became a thief in the Miller home, stealing our delight in and discovery of each of our children.

And it's not just basic toddler behavior that drives parents nuts. We have found sibling comparison to be a source of much frustration and agitation for our family. We try to avoid saying "Why can't you be more like your brother?" And we rationally know our children were made by God to be very different little people. But quite honestly, we still compare what we see them do differently and secretly wish one would act more like the other.

Analyn provides an everyday example of this.

Our sixth child, David, loves processes. He knows the drill every day when we walk in the door: Get your chores done, do your homework, clean your room, and then you may play with your friends. He does it almost without fail. Daniel, our youngest, also knows the drill but leaves his book bag, shoes, or coat (pretty much anything he brought to school that day) in the car, runs inside, and wants to be the first to turn on the television or play his games. After three or more reminders, he starts his chores and retrieves his backpack from the entryway floor or the car to start his homework.

"Early on my parents struggled to connect and empathize with us kids who are opposites of them. But I watched them become more understanding and accepting of those of us who are very different in terms of personality traits and strengths."

—CIERA (22)

These kids do this every day, and every day they respond to my instructions in their own ways. David strives to follow the process and make Mommy happy. Daniel is solely focused on being first, beating his brother. He is a little man on a mission, bound and determined to accomplish it.

Daniel's behavior can be frustrating, especially when it adds obstacles to getting multiple kids settled in the house after an outing. It can leave a mom thinking that very thing you aren't supposed to think: "Why can't he be good like his brother?" Frustration can lead me to raise my voice and direct looks of disapproval at the child who processes and responds differently. Comparison adds pressure and weight onto our children that they were not meant to carry. Frustration, whether sparked by comparison or flat-out poor behavior, is a very real parenting challenge.

Seeing the Who and Not the Do

Every parent knows that sometimes our emotions get the best of us. We say things we wish we could take back. Take a pause right now to consider this question: What happens when I become frustrated with someone, and what does it do to my perspective of that person?

Too easily, our frustration leads to statements that define another person inaccurately. What red flags can you identify in your own attitude and behavior to remind you that frustration has hijacked your parenting? For example, anytime we start a sentence with "You are…" and end it with a negative adjective, frustration has just led us somewhere we did not want to go with our children. Proverbs 15:4 says, "Kind words heal and help; cutting words wound and maim" (MSG). Our words can lead to wellness or to wounds.

We must guard against responding to frustration by wielding our powerful words in a way that defines our children solely by their present behavior. We want to consistently value and relate to our kids the way God does. So remember, when frustration enters the room, it's better to mute it than to give it the microphone. Otherwise, how can we expect to hear wisdom, direction, or creative solutions from God about how to respond to a concern? Parents aren't called to know everything; we are charged with the responsibility of learning, observing, learning some more, and leaning into God's guidance to usher children into their purpose.

L.R. Knost provides this helpful reminder in her book *The Gentle Parent*:

> The thing to remember is that parenting isn't about fixing a problem. It's about growing a person, and people have their own thoughts and opinions and ideas and plans, even when they are tiny people. Working with our children instead of against them creates a cooperative, teamwork dynamic as opposed to an adversarial, us-against-them atmosphere ripe for conflict.[1]

Frustration blocks our ability to understand our child. During seasons when one frustration seems to lead to another, we can ask questions like these: How well did I establish my expectations? Does my child need a current reminder of my expectations? We must ensure our expectations are clearly communicated and suitable for the age of the child. The surprising truth is that parenting is a collaborative process. We must learn to be *for* and *with* our kids. L.R. Knost continues,

> Parenting has nothing to do with perfection. Perfection isn't even the goal, not for us, not for our children. Learning together to live well in an imperfect world, loving each other despite or even because of our imperfections, and growing as humans while we grow our little humans, those are the goals of parenting.[2]

If we can leave you with one thing, it is this: See your child for who they are rather than what they do. Your child's identity matters more in the long haul than their behavior.

When frustration enters the room, it's better
to mute it than to give it the microphone.

As an adolescent, our third child, Ciera, challenged our patience. She confronted us with question after question, especially if she did not receive the answer she was looking for. Or she debated with us, using counterpoints and logic to get her way. The behavioral expression of her natural talents and hardwiring during adolescence could sometimes be frustrating and offensive, but a clear perspective of Ciera's identity revealed the powerhouse of a woman she would become. We learned to look past the momentary outbursts and recognize that if we became frustrated with Ciera, we would ultimately lose our connection with her. As we focused on the strengths of her character, we understood how to confront her challenging behavior in a way that led to constructive conversations.

Freedom to Stop Fixing

Frustration is to be expected and will come and go, but when it becomes our lingering companion, it will undermine and even destroy the thriving environment we are trying to foster in our homes. When it arises, we can pause to listen to what we know is true about our child before we start talking. This shifts us away from a performance- or behavior-based perspective and back to a clearer perspective. From here, it is much easier to speak words of encouragement.

See your child for who they are rather than what they do. Your child's identity matters more in the long haul than their behavior.

Every year, I (Brandon) attend the CliftonStrengths World Summit as a featured breakout speaker and connect with several colleagues who engage organizations, as I do, to shift their developmental strategy toward a strengths-based approach. As I was speaking with one of my "mates" from Australia, we got onto the topic of how we were learning so much by applying our professional knowledge to our parenting.

He shared about his nine-year-old son and the interest the boy has in design. In fact, even at nine, this little guy talked about someday being a designer for Disney. To encourage his son's talents and develop his strengths, my friend and his wife purchased a set of colored pens for him. One day, they were in their son's bedroom and noticed he had used the surface of his desk to mix some of the colors from his pen set to choose a design.

He went on to describe a scene most parents can relate to: He and his wife sat their son down and expressed their parental displeasure with his choice. My friend shook his head as he recalled the conversation, which focused on what their son had done wrong.

At this, I asked him a simple question: "What if you did the opposite?" Curious, he asked what I meant. I explained, "It's just a desk. Analyn and I don't typically encourage our kids to write on the furniture either, but what if you played to your son's strengths and allowed him to draw, design, and experiment *on* that desk? What if, years from now, your son could look at that desk or a photo of it and see how his dream started to take shape because you let him express his strengths—his art—in a unique way?"

With a tear forming in his eye, my colleague and friend expressed his gratitude for the shift in perspective and contemplated how he and his wife could play to their son's strength in a new way.

About a week later, I was delighted to receive a message from my friend featuring a photo and a brief note. There in full color was the image of a desk "decorated" with several drawings and intricate designs on the surface. Above it was the father's message: "We had a chat with our son about his desk. He's now started adding his creativity to it. Thanks for your coaching."

As we look for the shine in our child's eyes, we are not letting go of the need to establish standards and expectations in our home. My colleague and his wife were right to hold to the standard of not having their child draw on the furniture in his room. The concession was made after considering the unique case of this child, who stated he would like to be a designer. This is an important distinction as strengths-based parenting is not intended to lead to permissive or neglectful parenting. In fact, it is quite the opposite. Parenting from a strengths perspective is proactive and leads with strong standards and clear expectations for our kids.

Instead of "What did they do wrong and how do I fix them?" we can ask "Why did my child do this and how can I see their strengths in it?"

When we shift to a strengths-based focus, we open new possibilities to engage our children through a different filter. The questions change. Instead of "What did they do wrong, and how do I fix them?" we can ask "Why did my child do this, and how can I see their strengths in it?" We must maintain our commitment to who our child is so we aren't distracted by what they do. "Who is my child that they tend to act a certain way?" Stay in the discovery mode you employed in their first year of life. Restore the shine in your eyes and theirs by choosing to look beyond a moment or a behavior to see the uniquely and wonderfully wired child God has entrusted to you.

Grace in Parenting

In our home, when we started to notice who each child was as an individual, with abilities and gifts from God, we were freed to appreciate those strengths and focus on them. Our kids were released from living under a false formula that implied their performance and achievement determined our love for them. We had been Christians before this transformation; still, it took some time before we rested in grace.

Have you lived for a season of your life or your parenting with guilt and fear as stronger motivations than love and grace? Here is a verse to spend some time in.

> God is love. Whoever lives in love lives in God, and God in them. This is how love is made complete among us so that we will have confidence on the day of judgment: In this world we are like Jesus. There is no fear in love. But perfect love drives out fear, because fear has to do with punishment. The one who fears is not made perfect in love. We love because he first loved us (1 John 4:16-19).

This portion of Scripture is empowering for all parents. Notice that it says nothing about being the most punctual carpool parent or raising kids who are perfect specimens of humankind or hosting the ideal family dinner seven days a week. Our striving is not improving anyone's value. Only God's grace does that. It's true for you. It's true for your child.

These truths are about what we can do as loved children of God. We can love because God first loved us, and love drives out fear. Our fears and judgments do nothing to advance our children toward their purpose. God's got that covered. Our imperfect children have nothing to prove to us or to God to gain the identity of being God's loved handiwork.

Yes, we parents have responsibilities as caregivers and influencers, but the next time you are frustrated about or unforgiving of your child's behavior, trace that feeling back to its source. That source will be fear, not love. It will be guilt, not grace. When you make the intentional shift to parent from God's perspective of unconditional love and unlimited grace, you will see your child as God does. And your eyes, mouth, and heart will be quick to notice their strengths, not their weaknesses.

This transition did not happen overnight in our household; it happened as we responded to our kids and to our own parenting moments with fascination, forgiveness, and acceptance. We have often wondered, What if we had been more fascinated than frustrated when our first three kids were young? I know they would have benefited from the support. I am just thankful that we did finally start playing to their strengths before they left our home, and we encourage you with this: It is never too late to start seeing your kids, at any age or any stage, from this perspective.

This change has been a remarkable blessing to our family. We know this foundational shift can be the beginning of true transformation.

Restoring Relationships

To be clear, errors are still made and frustration is still present in the Miller home. However, now we watch for the red flag and move away from it before allowing ourselves to become angry. In anger, we say things we don't intend to say in a tone we don't intend to use. As parents, our words carry great weight in the hearts and minds of our children. It is imperative to be careful about how we speak into their lives; we should build them up, not tear them down. When you feel you have shifted from fascination to frustration and possibly even anger, remember the words of the apostle Paul to the Ephesians:

> "In your anger do not sin": Do not let the sun go down while you are still angry, and do not give the devil a foothold...Do not let any unwholesome talk come out of your mouths, but only what is helpful for building others up according to their needs, that it may benefit those who listen (Ephesians 4:26-29).

Holding on to anger produces reactions that are, at the least, not helpful and, at worst, injurious. When it comes to our children, it is helpful to keep short accounts with them. When they fail, when they offend, when they lie, when they steal, when they frustrate…we parents are instructed to let go of our anger, to be careful with the words we use, and to forgive them. We have found it helpful to hold our tongues rather than speaking something regrettable to our kids. Retreating to a place of prayer or stepping away from the situation long enough to regain composure helps us keep the right perspective of our children and reminds us of the important role we have in shaping their self-image. We do not want to "give the devil a foothold" by speaking something to our kids that will hurt their hearts and misshape their identities as dearly loved children.

However, with all our efforts to follow the words of Scripture and a sound parenting direction, we have said things to our kids that we regret. Can you relate? When we've spoken unwholesome words to our kids, we have found two important steps to take to restore the balance and reestablish right relationships with our children.

Acknowledge and Apologize

When we tear down our kids rather than build them up, it's important for us to acknowledge the wrong. Telling on ourselves to our children may seem counterintuitive, yet it establishes precedence in our home that even we, as loving parents, will occasionally fail in our efforts to lead our kids.

Acknowledgment of a wrong produces humility in us and ushers in the grace of God to restore the balance in our home. "He gives us more grace. That is why Scripture says: 'God opposes the proud but shows favor to the humble'" (James 4:6).

When parents acknowledge their mistake and offer a genuine apology, they give their children the opportunity to extend forgiveness. We have found our children, younger and older, are willing and glad to accept, forgive, and provide us grace to move forward when we fail. Instead of hearkening to the words spoken in anger, an apology provides the opportunity to reinforce our true and right perspective of our children. Obviously, the better choice, as we will read next, is to stay in discovery mode. However, when you become frustrated, acknowledging your error and making an apology go a long way toward building a foundation of integrity for your relationship with your children.

• • •

As we watch Lance's eyes light up each time he is with his son, my words for him are those I share with each parent I encounter: Don't ever stop being fascinated. Your child is God's handiwork.

———————— **REVIEW THE PLAY** ————————

1. What have you learned about yourself as a parent from this chapter's exploration?

2. What is one way this chapter helped you make a shift toward playing to your child's God-given strengths?

3. What did you discover about your child this week that surprises you or changes the way you interact with them?

4. Which insight or activity from this chapter's Playbook offering is the most helpful to your family right now? Why?

Check out the activities for chapter 2 in the Parenting Playbook on page 173.

3

Live in Discovery Mode

Everyone is born with certain talents. To develop
those talents, you have to know what they are.

MARY RECKMEYER

Relationships are all about connection. To stay connected with our children, we must stay in a mode of discovery. When you play to a child's strengths, you endeavor to see what is yet undiscovered and to unearth the hidden talents and gifting that define them.

> **discover** (*verb*): to learn, find out, or gain insight into something previously unseen or unknown

We can't be passive parents who sit by, hoping that somewhere along the road, the stars will align and our children will stumble onto a path of success and ease while avoiding major mistakes and bad decisions. Passivity and parenting just don't mix. We must get in the game and stay connected with our kids—not only when it's easy and exhilarating but also when it's hard and exhausting. We've been called and equipped by God to be one of the most prominent tools he will use to reveal himself and his plans to our children in their early years.

When you play to a child's strengths, you endeavor to see what is yet undiscovered and to unearth the hidden talents and gifting that define them.

The Gift of Discovery

When we stay in discovery mode, we are willing to learn who our child is as they grow and change through their lives. When our gaze shifts from our child and onto some ideal we have fancied in our minds of who they *should* be, we lose objectivity. We must fight to maintain a pure perspective of each of our children. Their futures depend on it. We will influence who they become more than anyone else in their lives. They absolutely pick up on the way we look at them, and they will define themselves accordingly—as a success or a disappointment, a source of pride or an embarrassment.

When we need a shift in perspective, the best place to seek wisdom and renewed vision is from the one who created our children. The Bible tells us that our children are wonderfully and intentionally created for good purposes by God. David expresses this in Psalm 139:

> You created my inmost being; you knit me together in my mother's womb. I praise you because I am fearfully and wonderfully made; your works are wonderful, I know that full well. My frame was not hidden from you when I was made in the secret place, when I was woven together in the depths of the earth. Your eyes saw my unformed body; all the days ordained for me were written in your book before one of them came to be. How precious to me are your thoughts, God! How vast the sum of them! Were I to count them, they would outnumber the grains of sand (verses 13-18).

If we focus primarily on our children's deficits, we may think they are set up for a future of hardship. But the truth is, God crafted them for a divine purpose. Ephesians 2:10 tells us that our children "are His workmanship, created in Christ Jesus for good works, which God prepared beforehand that [they] should walk in them" (NKJV). Our children and the world will benefit when we discover the unique ways God crafted our kids in order to propel them into the good plans God has for them. Your child's future is bright, and this parenting journey can be full of joy and excitement if you lean into the discovery process.

Here are three practical ways to stay in discovery mode, unearth the God-given uniqueness of your child, and play to their strengths:

1. Let them evolve.

2. Evaluate your why.

3. Learn their strengths.

These tactics, tested and tried in the Miller home, help us stay in discovery mode, keep frustration at bay, and preserve the shine in our own eyes through the daily grind of parenthood.

Let Them Evolve

You can open new opportunities for your kids by having them try things and seeing what makes their eyes light up. Be at peace with letting your children shift interests, and by all means, expose them to new experiences. As they are discovering who they are and what their passions are, you can either co-labor with or impede the process.

We aren't advocating for raising flighty kids. We teach our kids to finish what they start and honor their "yes," but we give them considerable leeway and the freedom to try, fail, and try again. Contribute to your children's growth rather than encouraging them to be stuck in one version and expression of themselves. Ask yourself questions like these: What's the next step in my child's growth and maturity? How do I help her get there? Who is my child growing into? Most of all, remember to focus your discovery primarily on the *who*, not what they *do*. Children develop a strong concept of self by knowing themselves internally, not by assessing their external achievements.

Our fifth child and youngest daughter, Madeline, has engaged in many extracurricular activities, including playing soccer, swimming, sewing, dancing, making pottery, baking, and cooking. Early on, Madeline really enjoyed athletics and played well for various teams. As she grew and matured, her interest in athletics waned, yet we found she was growing her love of cooking and baking. She took special interest in learning new recipes and sharing them with the family.

One day, Madeline was particularly inspired and made cream puffs. She presented these bakery-worthy creations to her mom. We were so pleased to learn that Madeline had taken it upon herself to look up the recipe and prepare the delectable yummies herself. When Madeline created a vison board (see page 175), she listed becoming a chef as one of her possible career choices. This is an example of allowing one of our children's interests to evolve as she matures and discovers who she is.

Just as marriage seminars remind us to grow with our spouses— letting our wife or husband change over time—we must extend that concept into our parenting strategy. Let your children change. Don't relate to a 25-year-old as the impetuous 15-year-old you remember. You might have to let go of a few beliefs or painful memories in order to see your child as an evolving masterpiece and move forward in this new relationship.

We must allow our kids to grow and make different choices. Their identities are not defined by their past failures or by our fear for their future. Just as God relates to us with grace, we can likewise reconcile old hurts with our children, creating forward momentum in our relationship with them. Second Corinthians 5:19 says, "God was reconciling the world to himself in Christ, not counting people's sins against them. And he has committed to us the message of reconciliation." We restore our connection with our children by seeing them in a new light.

Is there a painful memory you need to let go of to see your child as an evolving masterpiece?

Evaluate Your Why

The second key to staying in discovery mode is evaluating the why behind your parenting decisions. This involves taking a step back and honestly assessing your goal in the situation. Ask, "Am I leading my child to make me look good or to become their best self? Am I determining their best, or am I discovering what their best is? Am I being motivated by fear when I encourage my child to go this direction?" If the why points back to you—your identity, your expectations, your insecurities, or your plans—then halt and reevaluate. The objective *is not* to create a Mini-Me who responds, decides, and operates in life like you do. Nor is it to mold and build an impressive little achiever who reflects well on you. Instead, recognize that you are powerfully positioned to guide your children in the discovery process of becoming who they are meant to be.

In his book *Start with Why*, Simon Sinek explains, "People don't buy WHAT you do; they buy WHY you do it."[1] Children are smart, and as they age, they become smarter. We have learned, sometimes through trial and error, that our children can see right through our motives. Sinek advises, "For those who have an open mind for new ideas, who seek to create long-lasting success and who believe that your success requires the aid of others, I offer you a challenge. From now on, Start with Why."[2]

When we were young parents, we dressed, prepped, and prompted our children to behave a certain way to make us look good in public. In this "what first" approach to parenting, our primary concern was, What will people think of us as parents if our children are not perfectly behaved and impeccably groomed? As sad as it is to admit, we bribed our children with sweets or special amusements to modify their behavior. And our kids picked up on the game—rather quickly in fact. As we upped the ante with our bribes, their behavior seemed to worsen proportionately.

As our parenting philosophy began to shift, we approached family outings much differently. We began to see it was far more important to focus first on the why behind our parenting approach instead of the what. The old way involved dressing, prepping, and promoting a certain type of behavior we wanted to see—and providing the corresponding incentives to obtain that conduct. The new approach was focused on always encouraging positive behavior in our children.

We also sought to understand the differences among our children. Which ones had a shorter attention span? Which children needed extra supervision because they were prone to wander? Which children needed a nap? Which children began to struggle if they were hungry? As Sinek goes on to say, "Knowing your WHY is not the only way to be successful, but it is the only way to maintain a lasting success and have a greater blend of innovation and flexibility."[3]

As we invested our time and care into really knowing our children, our conversations about why it was important to behave well in public became more natural. We taught them that being considerate of others was a family value. We then modeled this behavior when we interacted with others and with them, and we encouraged them to follow our example. Our clear reasons for acting properly in public produced far better results and significantly less frustration than incentives ever could.

John Quincy Adams nicely summed up the qualities of a leader: "If your actions inspire others to dream more, learn more, do more and become more, you are a leader." Consider this as your *why*—your objective in every challenging parenting choice you make. Remember Zander's compelling question for parents: "Who am I being that my child's eyes are not shining?" Take a moment and honestly consider whether your *why* is inspiring a course of action that brightens the shine in your child's eyes.

Learn Their Strengths

The third crucial key to staying in discovery mode and helping children become authentic, fulfilled adults is to learn their strengths. When the late Donald O. Clifton, the father of strengths psychology, was in graduate school, he asked, "What would happen if we studied what was right with people versus what's wrong with people?"[4] Then for 40 years he focused on that very discovery. His message was that we could help develop people by focusing on their natural talents instead of trying to cure them of their weaknesses. So many offerings and perspectives in the world teach us to focus on fixing the wrong rather than identifying what's right. As Clifton emphasizes, "The real tragedy of life is not that each of us doesn't have enough strengths, it's that we fail to use the ones we have. Benjamin Franklin called wasted strengths, 'sundials in the shade.'"[5] We foster confidence and capability in our children when we identify and then play to their strengths.

Throughout much of this book, we'll share examples of how we have applied this key in our family and witnessed transformational results. Focusing on the strengths of our children means we are constantly discovering all that is right with our kids, helping them see it in themselves, and developing those talents accordingly. The philosophy of focusing on strengths is not difficult to understand, yet it is challenging to master. Consider one of the areas where we have been conditioned to focus on weakness instead of strength—the education system.

When Madeline brought home her sixth-grade report card, her grades looked like this:

Reading	A+
Math	C
Science	A–
Art	A–
PE	A
Social Studies	B

Like most parents, when we first glanced at this report card, we were drawn to the C in math. In fact, I show this report card to business groups all over the United States and ask the participants which grade they are drawn to first, and almost every time, the answer is the C. Why are we drawn to this grade first? Personally, I mentally highlight the lower grade because I was a strong performer in school, and even as a kid, I would have looked at my own report card with scrutiny. So that judgment is built in from my childhood priorities and strengths as an honor roll student. My natural expectation for my children is for them to perform the same way.

Focusing on the strengths of our children means
we are constantly discovering all that is right
with our kids, helping them see it in themselves,
and developing those talents accordingly.

Most people would view the math grade as the greatest opportunity for improvement. And a logical assumption is that this is the subject area in which Madeline has the greatest potential to see measurable progress. But what if this perspective is wrong? When Madeline presented her report card to us, we were about to ask her about the C. Thankfully, we switched gears at the last second and asked Madeline about the A+ in reading. Our talk unfolded with great joy and connection.

Brandon: "Maddie, you received an A+ in reading. Great job, sweetheart! Do you really like to read?"

Maddie: "Oh, Daddy, I love to read! Sometimes you and Mommy think I am in my room sleeping, but I'm not. (Said with a special twinkle in her eyes.) Sometimes I stay up till two in the morning reading!"

Brandon: "Wow, you really like to read that much?"

Maddie: "Uh-huh!"

Brandon: "Well, I tell you what. This summer, I'm going to give you a special job. You have an unlimited allowance to purchase books…with one requirement: Every book you purchase, you agree to read the book and write a summary for me. For every book that's 100 pages or longer, I will pay you a dollar. For every book that's 200 pages or more, I will pay you two dollars, and for every book 300 pages or more, I will pay you five dollars."

Maddie: "You're going to pay me to read?"

Me: "Yes. As long as your book reports are turned in every Monday in the format we agree to, you will get paid."

What do you think happened over the summer? If you guessed that our wallets became a lot lighter, you are correct. Madeline read book after book after book. It was interesting to notice that she required very little prompting to read the books she selected. In fact, she took the initiative herself to make sure she read the books and turned in the summaries on time. Another interesting result occurred: Over the summer, the quality of her book reports began to improve. By the end of the summer, both her reading fluency and her comprehension significantly advanced.

Most of us are conditioned to believe that the greatest advancement and the worthiest improvement is when a C turns into an A. But what if the most important room for growth happens when we build up a strength and make it possible for an A+ to become a figurative A+++? Before we can parent to the strengths of our children, we must become active students of our children.

With diligence and commitment, we watched for moments when a talent became apparent in one of our kids, and then we tested the truth of that evaluation over time. Remaining in discovery mode is very intentional. When we watch for shining eyes, the red flag of frustration, opportunities for our children to evolve, and moments to evaluate our why, we can more readily see and appreciate strengths instead of focusing on weaknesses.

Before we can parent to the strengths of our children,
we must become active students of our children.

Parenting Without Regrets

Do you know the number one regret of the dying? It is this: "I wish I'd had the courage to live a life true to myself, not the life others expected of me."[6]

I (Analyn) was a 17-year-old mother, so people had certain ideas about how my life would turn out. In their minds, the bar was set low. Statistically, having a child at that young age diminished my options for the future. As our young family grew in those early years of our marriage, I had to decide—would I allow the voices of doubters to penetrate my thoughts or would I tune in to the voice of my heavenly Father, who promised me he had a perfect plan for my life?

This question constantly brought me back to a place of hope and trust. God had designed me with unique talents. I could trust his leading and, with hard work and determination, see a future path with incredible potential. This is the courage I seek to inspire in our children—to live devoted to their heavenly Father, trusting he has a perfect plan for their lives and to hold on to the promise of courage to overcome every obstacle in the path to success.

We want to help our children live their version of a great life. Perfection in parenting is not the antidote to regret, nor are good intentions. It is the synergy between our beliefs and our choices that lead us toward a sense of accomplishment at the end of our days. We believe God has brilliantly crafted our children for good purposes in this world. Every day we try to teach our kids how to make decisions based on their faith and their unique strengths to live an authentic and responsible life. Dr. Mary Reckmeyer, daughter of Donald Clifton, offers this encouragement in her book *Strengths Based Parenting*:

> As a parent you can encourage your children in hundreds of ways, and there are hundreds of things for you to worry about and wonder about. Yet even in the midst of your busy and complex daily schedule, you have the opportunity to focus on your children in a way that will have a lasting and positive impact on their lives. You can appreciate their individuality. You can help them see and know their natural affinities—their talents that can become strengths. You can help them explore their interests. And you can build your life—and their lives—on what will help them become productive, happy people.[7]

When you stay in discovery mode, your expectations will support rather than hinder your kids' journeys to become their best selves in God. You can teach children how to let go of other people's expectations and courageously find their own path, full of adventure and fulfillment. When you do this, you can parent through the years without regret, having accomplished the goal of helping your children discover how to walk in their purpose.

—————————— **REVIEW THE PLAY** ——————————

1. What have you learned about yourself as a parent from this chapter's exploration?

2. What is one way this chapter helped you make a shift toward playing to your child's God-given strengths?

3. What did you discover about your child this week that surprises you or changes the way you interact with them?

4. Which insight or activity from this chapter's Playbook offering is the most helpful to your family right now? Why?

Check out the activities for chapter 3 in the Parenting Playbook on page 175.

4

Identify and Honor
Their Strengths

*Everyone is a genius. But if you judge a fish on its ability to
climb a tree, it will live its whole life believing that it is stupid.*

OFTEN ATTRIBUTED TO ALBERT EINSTEIN

Recently, David came home from school with a note from his
teacher. While penned with the best of intentions, the teacher's
statement was in complete contrast to our parenting philosophy: "I
hope to make your lives a little easier by helping you identify your
child's deficits so you can better assist him to overcome them and so
your son might experience even better success."

People commonly rely on deficit identification as a path to excellence or success. This truth hit home at our house when we received
that note from David's teacher. We fully believe this teacher wants
the best for our son, but the note underscores the difference between
the teacher's approach to personal development and ours. Dr. Clifton
once told his son, Jim, "Your weaknesses will never develop, while your
strengths will develop infinitely."[1] Our children's innate talents have the
potential to become their life-defining strengths.

So how do parents start unearthing these talents? We look at our
kids with curiosity to know who God meant for them to become.

What do we see in them? What potential exists that we should be resourcing and developing? As we said before, it is not a great mystery. God meant for you and your child to be clear about how he has crafted them and their purpose.

As you watch for a child's natural, God-given abilities, you will likely notice two levels of strength, which we call "shining strength" and "secondary strength."

Our kids' primary, dominant, and most noticeable strengths are the shining strengths. These abilities and tendencies shine forth in our kids and hold the greatest potential for their success, impact, and contentment. The secondary strengths can also lead to success and become dominant areas of ability and service—but only with more involved inquiry and commitment to development.

You likely have noticed the beginnings of a secondary strength in your child. For example, let's say your daughter hesitates to get in front of people to speak, yet when she is placed in a situation that requires her to be a leader or share with a group, she has a captivating way of engaging her audience. Public speaking is likely a secondary strength. Her ease and her shining strength emerge when she crosses over to connecting with people. With practice and experience, that daughter's shining and secondary strengths will merge with ease rather than frustration, creating more chances for her to use her shining strength of relating to and engaging others. This is a great example of how a shining strength can make up for a lesser strength.

Strengths expert and author Michael Dauphinee offers this perspective in his book *Extraordinary*: "People who understand their identity, move toward it, and are given opportunities to express it day to day live more emotionally engaged lives."[2]

Start identifying shining and secondary strengths in your children. As you remain fascinated with your kids and commit to nurturing their abilities, this practice becomes the basis for enabling them to live emotionally engaged lives and enjoy greater levels of confidence.

The Five E's of Strength Identification

To empower you for this task, we've created an easy way to notice a child's strengths. Both the shining strengths and the secondary strengths will be evident when you watch for the Five E's of strength identification:

enthusiasm

ease

excellence

energy

enjoyment

We'll walk through these. As you consider each one and the snapshot examples we've provided, notice which of your child's abilities and areas of interest come to mind. These will help you move from fascination to identification and prepare you for the all-important stage of validation. You won't merely be cheering for your child's strengths; you will be validating them through your priorities, your family's activities and pursuits, and your words of encouragement.

Enthusiasm

enthusiasm (*noun*): an absorbing or controlling possession of the mind by any interest or pursuit; lively interest

Enthusiasm is hard to miss. You can see it in your children's eyes, hear it in their tone of voice, and witness it in their actions. To help you notice your child's enthusiasm, here are some questions to consider:

- What is your kid naturally drawn to?
- What do they enjoy and why?
- What is it about the activity that captures their attention?

We have kids who love to play video games, so we ask ourselves, What is it about the problem solving, the winning, and the challenge that draws them to it? In the same way, identify your own child's enthusiasm toward something. Watch their eyes light up as they read, play a sport, create something with their hands, or engage with a subject in school. Use this response as a barometer of enthusiasm and then pay attention.

A Snapshot of Enthusiasm

David loves to watch programs that involve intrigue and suspense. As he watches these shows, he tries to figure out the plot and see if he can work out how the show will end. David demonstrates this enthusiasm every week by reminding us to make sure certain programs are set to be recorded just in case he is unable to watch them live.

Ease

> **ease** (*noun*): freedom from difficulty or great effort

Some things just come to us easily. We seem to see the steps as though the activity was tailor-made for us to engage with. As you observe your child, ask yourself questions like these:

- What comes to my child easily?
- Is there a subject matter or activity that they have picked up quickly?
- What does my child seem to innately know the steps to or effortlessly engage in?

Maybe you have a child who is drawn to baking. You come home and find them in the kitchen mixing ingredients. You see their creativity and skill pouring out as they try new recipes.

Or maybe your child is the one who picks up a pair of sticks and starts to "play drums," naturally keeping time and rhythm. Keep a keen eye for ease and rapid learning in your child.

A Snapshot of Ease

When Michaela, our fourth child, began playing soccer at age six, she started with an older age group so she could play with her cousin. In her first game, she intuitively understood the nuances of the game and easily scored the first goal of the season. From there, Michaela seemed to always know where to position herself on the field to make the best play. As her soccer experience progressed, Michaela's coaches consistently trusted her to be a "smart" player on the field. She easily absorbs knowledge of the game, and her strength is honed with each practice and game.

Excellence

---

excellence (*noun*): the fact or state of excelling; superiority; eminence

---

To truly be excellent, third-party validation is required. It's not enough for us to see our kids engage in an activity and assign excellence to their efforts. Earning top marks, winning first place in a contest, or having the rest of the family call out the top-notch performance would be evidence of excellence. Here are some questions to consider as you watch for excellence:

- Where do you see a standout ability separating them from average engagement and aptitude?
- Who has validated their performance?
- What awards have they earned for outstanding performance?

Being enthusiastically drawn to something and doing it with ease does not necessarily equate to excellence. We can enjoy things but not be particularly great at them—those are called hobbies. But often when an activity evokes enthusiasm, ease, and excellence that are validated by others, it very well could be showcasing your child's emerging strength. Now you've pinpointed a talent to maximize and invest in.

A SNAPSHOT OF EXCELLENCE

Our son-in-law Adam (Ciera's husband) is a Major League Baseball enthusiast. As a child, Adam played for travel baseball teams and excelled as a pitcher. He was often counted on to pitch several innings for his teams and thrived with high velocity and pinpoint accuracy. In high school, Adam was well on his way to earning a scholarship before an arm injury changed his prospects. These days, he serves as a coach for travel teams and has an eye for talented pitchers. He loves to cultivate young people's strengths and is often hired to provide private lessons to up-and-coming players. Adam has turned his passion for baseball into excellence as a sought-after coach.

Energy

> **energy** (*noun*): the capacity for vigorous activity; available power

Energy is a tremendous indicator of talent in our kids. We can measure their energy level before an activity and check again after the fact. When natural talent is present, activities will energize us. We might be depleted from the exertion, but we still feel empowered to engage even more. Consider these questions about your child's energy:

- What energizes your child?
- What activities leave your child depleted?
- When does your kid seem to exhibit an endless reserve of energy?

Take a moment to consider this for yourself—that may help you more easily recognize it in your child. I'm energized by speaking to a crowd. I walk away from an all-day speaking engagement jazzed. I may be physically tired, but my mind is buzzing, my eyes are shining, and I am excited to wake up and do it again tomorrow. I am energized by doing what I was made to do.

Now, I want to make an important point here. Your child may walk away from an activity feeling energized, but that doesn't necessarily mean they have mastered it yet. Mastery will come with development.

But seeing your child energized by an activity clues you in to an emerging talent.

A SNAPSHOT OF ENERGY

Our daughter-in-law, Christine (Lance's wife), is energized by serving people. As we watch her with her husband and son, she seems to have limitless energy to serve them and care for their needs. Whenever we have family gatherings, Christine is consistently looking for ways to serve our family members. She takes great delight in helping her younger siblings as well as us parents. When we travel or need a second set of hands to help us with the kids, Christine is willing and ready to pitch in, and although I'm sure she gets run down like anyone else, she seems to derive energy and satisfaction from serving others. When we started a youth group in our home, Christine volunteered to help us. She is such a natural with teens and looks strong as she engages them with fun activities and small-group discussions. She epitomizes the snapshot of energy, as after each youth group night, she is already thinking about what can be done the following week to make the experience meaningful and enjoyable.

"Before I found out what my top strengths were, I was somewhat lost as far as what career path to choose, let alone what I would be good at. Once I found out that my top strengths revolved around understanding people, relating to people, and empathizing with people, management and coaching people was my career of choice, and I have not looked back since."

—ADAM (CIERA'S HUSBAND) (23)

Enjoyment

> **enjoyment** (*noun*): a particular form or source of pleasure

Enjoyment is a crucial component to talent development. Enjoyment is the fulfillment of a job well done. It's a win, a successful outcome, or a grade accomplished. Enjoyment is evident in satisfaction as well as in resilience. Here are a couple of questions to consider for observing enjoyment:

- When your child completes tasks or projects or assignments, which ones seem to give them the greatest satisfaction?

- What does your child enjoy so much that they will press through difficulties to do it?

- Which activities does your child take the most pride in accomplishing?

Grit is one of the most important traits we can foster in our children as they are identifying their talents and turning them into strengths. This ability to press through even when things get hard will allow true strengths to mature. Passion married with perseverance is key to long-term success in students. When your child displays enjoyment both in the win and in the battle to succeed—when grit becomes part of the equation—you have found a talent that can move into the realm of strengths.

A Snapshot of Enjoyment

When our son-in-law Jordan (Bailee's husband) is learning a new song to play on the drums, he spends the time and energy required to master a riff. He has told us of times when as a young person, he would practice so long, his hands would bleed from the constant pounding of the drums to get the beat just right. When we asked if this pain deterred him, he told us he forgot the pain as soon as he accomplished his goal. This is what enjoyment looks like. We can see our kids push through pain for the pleasure of the accomplishment.

From personal experience and loads of research, we wholeheartedly believe that identifying talents rather than deficits in your child holds the key to their success.

Identifying Your Kids' Strengths

Strengths are not elusive when we learn how and where to find them. The Five E's equip us with a framework to guide our exploration of our children's natural strengths and provide clues to new strengths we uncover as our kids grow and mature. The key is to stay in discovery mode with our kids and commit to continually uncover their unique strengths.

Identifying talents rather than deficits in your child holds the key to their success.

To aid in the discovery process, I (Brandon) developed an inventory of strengths for you to consider as you investigate the Five E's for your child. This inventory of strengths is available to you on our website, www.analynbrandon.com. This inventory of strengths is based on years of observation with our own children as well as insights I have gained over 15 years working with individuals and organizations as a strengths-based development expert. By no means is this list meant to be exhaustive. It will, however, provide you with a jumping-off point to begin your process of discovery and development.

In the Parenting Playbook, we provide you with further instructions for how to identify the top strengths in your kids. After reading the rest of this chapter, turn to pages 179–180, where we provide you with further instructions on how to identify the top strengths in your kids.

The Impact at Home

The ideal home environment elevates the human potential of each family member, pointing to everyone's unique strengths and warring against the expression of self-doubt and negativity. One of the key attributes of a strengths-based home culture is celebration. Identifying and celebrating the strengths of your child changes the atmosphere in your home.

Find every excuse to celebrate one another. Call out the strengths you see at work in your family. As parents, we set the tone of our homes, and we have the power to create an environment where our uniquely wired children can flourish. Fill your dinner table conversations with positive words that cheer up and encourage rather than criticize and cast doubt.

Identifying and celebrating the strengths of your child changes the atmosphere in your home.

We are excited that you are well on your way to creating a home that nurtures your child and God's purpose and strength in your child.

A Tale of Two Sisters

We want to tell you a tale about the two oldest Miller sisters, Bailee and Ciera. (We have the benefit of built-in case studies about a strengths-focused home!) When the sisters were young, they both participated in musical theater. We loved watching our girls perform and develop their talents. One year, Bailee and Ciera performed together in the musical *Into the Woods*. Bailee played Jack's mom, and Ciera performed as Jack. It was fascinating to watch the two characters because they mirrored our girls' personalities and strengths. Jack's mom was careful, pragmatic, and more interested in preserving her good nature and well-being. Jack was whimsical, outgoing, optimistic, and a seeker of good fortune. We had a lot of fun noting the similarities to our two girls.

Though the sisters shared the stage, they—and we—were reminded they didn't share the same strengths. They were beginning to discover their respective emerging talents. At the same time, we were watching this dynamic and becoming clued in on the talents that would some-day become their strengths.

In the next two chapters, we'll explore how the Five E's became evident in the lives of these two very different sisters and how the girls' strengths blossomed. Their stories become living examples of how playing to a child's strengths can highlight purpose and potential influence. We hope you'll be encouraged as you begin to incorporate these parenting principles in your home and with your child.

—————————— **REVIEW THE PLAY** ——————————

1. What have you learned about yourself as a parent from this chapter's exploration?

2. What is one way this chapter helped you make a shift toward playing to your child's God-given strengths?

3. What did you discover about your child this week that surprises you or changes the way you interact with them?

4. Which insight or activity from this chapter's Playbook offering is the most helpful to your family right now? Why?

Check out the activities for chapter 4 in the Parenting Playbook on page 179.

Uncover Their Calling
(Ciera's Tale)

*Our chief want is someone who will inspire
us to be what we know we could be.*

RALPH WALDO EMERSON

Y ou have front-row seats to witness and appreciate your child's beauty and gifting. Which means you also know how tough it is to parent when your kid's lack of maturity and development undermines their strengths and creates obstacles and pain.

We have some good news for you. We've discovered that some of the best moments for teaching and encouragement occur when children are not at their best. When parents come alongside a child during a season of struggle, the result can be amazing. Every child can learn more about themselves and how their strengths relate to their calling. You'll witness what this looks like as we pay attention to Ciera and Bailee's paths in this chapter and the next.

We'll start with Ciera and explore how her phases of discovery unfolded, why embracing a calling is for everyone, and how our attention to the Five E's of strengths identification kept us true to her strengths journey even when we had doubts.

Shaping Raw Strengths

Early on, we could see that Ciera was a natural leader. She's always been outspoken, with a strong will, strong opinions, and the ability to lead others toward a goal. Those strengths, when displayed immaturely, turn people off. And they did. Ciera's freshman year, she ran for class president. Despite her unmistakable presence and uninhibited drive to succeed, she did not win. It was a tough day in our house as she recounted how her classmates said they didn't vote for her because she was sometimes too bossy.

In 2014, Sheryl Sandberg, COO of Facebook and author of *Lean In*, started a "ban bossy" campaign because she had experienced and was still seeing the way that word squelches leadership in girls. I think Sandberg hits on a great point. We don't want to mute our daughters for fear of them being labeled bossy when what we are actually seeing is the raw material of a leader within. She states, "Leadership is the expectation that you can use your voice for good. That you can make the world a better place."[1] Our role as parents is to help our children become all that God intended them to be.

Consider the biblical story of Esther. She was strengthened to be a leader of her people. God's plan was to use her presence, position, and speech to save her people. When she was called on to stand up to the king, her cousin Mordecai encouraged her,

> If you remain silent at this time, relief and deliverance for the Jews will arise from another place, but you and your father's family will perish. And who knows but that you have come to royal position for such a time as this? (Esther 4:14).

Esther is being reminded that she has been given a voice at a specific time, and her choice to boldly step into that opportunity could mean life or death for her family. She was positioned and equipped with strength to be the woman God made her to be. We see our Ciera in a similar way. She is gifted and positioned to bring her strengths to her generation in "such a time as this." Our job is to help her develop talents in a way that brings life to those around her. Your job is to help your child manifest their God-given strengths with maturity and purpose.

Refine and Redirect

After Ciera's election loss and experience with rejection, we had the challenge of consoling her while also showing her how to leverage her talent in a way that would prove effective and beneficial for those around her. God doesn't give us a strength to serve only ourselves. He wants us to use our abilities to serve him and his children.

Over time, we talked about the beauty in Ciera's strength as well as the importance of tuning in to the people around her, using tact, and connecting with an audience, not merely commanding them. We teach these life lessons more than once, and that's okay.

We encouraged Ciera to look at other avenues beyond student government to engage her talents. She found her new stage in athletics and joined the cheer squad and track team. She excelled athletically and brought her unmistakable presence to the teams. As her sophomore year approached, Ciera passionately embarked on a second attempt to run for class president. We encouraged her to campaign to her best ability and whispered some reminders about ways leaders effectively connect with followers.

She gave her speech, the votes were tallied, and Ciera lost again. She was devastated. The losses were eating away at her self-image, and we could see our girl struggling in the weeks and months that followed. Ciera found herself in a bit of a transition. She had some challenges during her freshman year and needed to make some choices about how she wanted to conduct herself and what role she wanted faith to play in her life.

Staying in line with our commitment to emphasize strengths rather than weaknesses, we discussed with Ciera how and where she could invest her energy and develop her talent. She continued to redirect where she was applying her strengths—not because we believed she shouldn't be in leadership (quite the opposite). We didn't want her to lose hope in that possibility by giving up. She merely needed to reconsider where and how to refine her strengths while she was maturing into her calling.

Compelled by a Calling

You are blessed with the privilege of finding out how your child will ultimately express their talents in their calling. Many people refer to a calling only in terms of a ministry, a place where our kids will ultimately serve the Lord. But we consider a calling to be a lifestyle, not a gift to be defined by categories such as ministry, career, and family. Our kids are equipped with talents and passions that God has integrated into the fabric of their being and that will compel them through all areas of life.

Have you looked at your children through the lens of their calling? It really does change things, especially when you broaden the understanding beyond one area or one role in your kid's life. When your child is texting during church or tattling on a sibling, you can know that your patience with her and your focus on and investment in her strengths matters.

Our children are not perfect, but they are sustained and guided by Jesus, the perfecter of their faith (Hebrews 12:2). The good and influential work of their life will emerge and mature. Every child of God has a calling on their life—their full life. This perspective can radically change your heart and your family. Your child will become compelled by a sense of calling, and you will be compelled to be present as an encourager, teacher, observer, listener, and influencer.

We know that Ciera's hardwiring is who she is in every facet of her life. This is why we asked her some big questions in the midst of her rebellion and transitional times, questions like these:

- What kind of person do you want to be?
- What do you want to be known for?
- How do you want others to describe you?

It was a pivotal time for her to draw closer to her calling. Over time, she came to a place where—between her and God—she realized she wanted to become a charismatic leader who uses her gift to serve and inspire others to lead impactful lives. This empowered her to say no to some behavior and other relationships. It inspired her to say yes to certain extracurricular and volunteer opportunities.

As Ciera became open to new ways of walking in her strengths, one of her teachers noticed she had a knack for presenting publicly and encouraged her to enter a Poetry Out Loud contest. Ciera entered, prepared, and in fact won the competition! She then competed in and won several more Poetry Out Loud contests.

Our children are not perfect, but they are sustained and guided by Jesus, the perfecter of their faith.

One day, Ciera heard the names of the winners of the school's mock trial team announced over the school intercom. Naturally, she wanted to be a winner too, so she decided to try out for the team with a good friend. Mock trial was well suited to Ciera's strengths because it is similar to debate but in a courtroom context. She tried out and made the team, but now her time was being divided among too many activities. She chose to divert her energy toward mock trial, where she experienced great success. Her confidence and self-image soared.

At the end of the year, she decided to run for junior class treasurer. Even with all her effort and growth in public speaking, the election results came out the same—she lost for a third time. However, this time, as we consoled our daughter, we found a more mature Ciera. She reasoned that she wasn't yet ready to be in the lead role and accepted an appointed position on the associated student body (ASB) council as the academic awards commissioner. There she would be able to make a difference as a leader of a specific committee.

This was one of the best things that could have happened in Ciera's leadership development journey. The ups and downs of working on a team presented opportunities for us to discuss leadership principles and styles and how people interact, react, and contribute differently. She noticed unique talents in her peers and appreciated differing strengths. Our conversations and this real-life experience empowered Ciera to look at her natural tendencies, the needs of others, and ways to develop her own leadership style.

When our focus is no longer on winning but on serving and living

"The benefit of focusing on my strengths clicked for me when I was in high school. That's when I learned what God made me good at and I began to use my strengths to glorify him. When I was the captain of the mock trial team and student body president, I often consulted my father on how to deal with situations and how to lead to the best of my ability. Knowing my strengths enabled me to jump into my calling at a very young age."

—CIERA (22)

out a calling, we are compelled by a pure and purposed motivation.

"Try, Try Again"...Takes a Team

At the end of Ciera's sophomore year, our family had begun a youth ministry in our home. This gave Ciera an opportunity to invite classmates into her home to learn biblical teaching and grow in a community of faith. Ciera had matured in her faith and in her communication skills, so she was able share her testimony with other students. What a joy to watch kids come to faith at Ciera's invitation to receive Jesus as their Lord and Savior.

Something shifted in our daughter when she applied her strengths in a ministry context and saw how lives could be impacted. As John C. Maxwell says, "A leader's credibility begins with personal success. It ends with helping others achieve personal success."[2]

Ciera recognized that her leadership gift was meant to produce more than wins and personal success. She saw the eternal significance of serving others with her strengths. As Ciera's junior year came to an end, she announced she was going to run for the ASB president position. Honestly, after witnessing her disappointment during each of the previous three years, we tried to talk her out of it. We realize this wasn't one of our prouder moments, but we wanted to spare our daughter the potential pain of losing again. So Ciera asked her school counselor to help convince us to support her decision to run again. Funny thing is, her counselor was the same counselor who worked there when Analyn and I attended the school. Needless to say, we capitulated to her request and allowed Ciera to run.

Parent to parent, we encourage you to push back against the

temptation to "pull up the tent stakes" when your kids experience hardship and failure. It is brutal to watch and even worse for your kids to endure. Fighting through momentary battles typically produces long-term victories. Giving a child the time and space to find and grow toward their calling is well worth the effort and the missteps.

You see, in addition to developing our kids' natural talents, God is up to something else. He is developing their character. As Paul writes in Romans, "We also glory in our sufferings, because we know that suffering produces perseverance; perseverance, character; and character, hope. And hope does not put us to shame" (5:3-5). In ease and in hardship, we are partnering with God as he forms our children's character and ultimately prepares them for the life he has called them to.

It can feel like walking through a maze, watching for signs of talent and knowing when to encourage perseverance and when to prompt a child to change their direction. But we are led by the Spirit of God, and he gives wisdom generously to every parent who asks for it. James writes, "If any of you lacks wisdom, you should ask God, who gives generously to all without finding fault, and it will be given to you" (1:5).

In ease and in hardship, we are partnering with God as he forms our children's character and ultimately prepares them for the life he has called them to.

You and your child are not in this alone. Your family's awareness and prayerful discernment will turn the try-try-again times into trust-again times to lean into God and toward a calling. A child will remember these experiences of depending on Jesus the next time failure or discouragement tempts them (or you) to give up.

The Fruit of Maturity

In Ciera, God was developing humility, kindness, and consideration for others. God wasn't withholding opportunities from Ciera in the midst of her failure; he was, in fact, creating space for her to grow in a fullness of character that would inform her leadership in the future. The appointed position on the student body and the youth ministry environment both were beautiful gifts from God in her leadership journey. If we had pulled up the stakes too soon and not allowed her to experience failure and exercise grit as she persevered, it would have been to her detriment. As Maxwell goes on to state, "Being who you are is the first step in becoming better than you are."[3]

The senior year election went differently—Ciera was elected ASB president! In this role, she leveraged all the lessons from the prior three years and served her classmates.

We rejoice in Ciera's successes and celebrate her determination to overcome adversity and immaturity as she pursued her passion for student government. The entire process, not just the victory, was significant. An emerging calling becomes the catalyst for more mature decisions and endeavors. Purpose, not success, becomes a sincere motivation for your child.

The Five E's in Action

The activities in your child's life will change over time, but the intrinsic talents won't.

We relied on the Five E's to identify and encourage Ciera's God-given talents without being overly focused on one activity, such as sports, theater, poetry, or debate. We were clued in to our daughter's identity through her apparent *enthusiasm* toward speaking, which became evident when she became involved in theater. It was *easy* for Ciera to walk onto a stage and begin speaking. It was easy for her to memorize lines. She was *energized* about every opportunity to step out and speak. We saw *excellence* emerge when she entered the poetry competitions. Her talents brought her victories, and she was hooked!

Despite three years in a row of campaign losses, Ciera was not deterred from running again. Was she a glutton for failure? No. In fact, the opposite was true—she could not shake her love for leading and communicating. Even when she didn't do it well, she *enjoyed* leading so much, she was willing to risk pain to go for it again. As Winston Churchill once said, "No boy or girl should ever be disheartened by lack of success in their youth but should diligently and faithfully continue to persevere and make up for lost time."[4] Failure was not final because Ciera displayed perseverance. She fought through it and was willing to grow, develop, learn, and try again because she found a level of deep satisfaction from her successes. When Ciera won a poetry competition or saw a peer come to faith, her *enjoyment* level was off the charts! That joy exceeded the pain of past failures.

As she slowly uncovered her calling, Ciera's grit sustained her and compelled her to keep pressing on to become who she knew (and we so clearly saw) God made her to be.

—————————— REVIEW THE PLAY ——————————

1. What have you learned about yourself as a parent from this chapter's exploration?

2. What is one way this chapter helped you make a shift toward playing to your child's God-given strengths?

3. What did you discover about your child this week that surprises you or changes the way you interact with them?

4. Which insight or activity from this chapter's Playbook offering is the most helpful to your family right now? Why?

Check out the activities for chapter 5 in the Parenting Playbook on page 183.

6

Activate the Ripple Effect (Bailee's Tale)

Confidence is instilled, not inherited.

SCOTT HAGAN

As we raised two daughters close in age and vastly different in gifting, we knew one thing above all else—our goal was not to turn Bailee into Ciera or Ciera into Bailee. If each girl was the standard of success for the other, they would fail miserably. Instead, we saw something unique and lovely in each of them.

Bailee, our bashful girl who struggled with stage fright and was often too shy to even purchase a trinket from a store clerk, has become a worship leader who sings with confidence and sincerity from the stage at church. Talk about a transformation! It took some time, self-discovery, and trial and error, but Bailee eventually experienced an amazing collision of talent and passion that mitigated her weaknesses and propelled her forward into her strengths. We'll look at how transformation happens not by focusing on weaknesses but by focusing on strengths and areas of interest. We'll see how a person who knows their purpose, grows their potential, and sows to serve others will set off a ripple of influence for the rest of their life.

Raising World Changers

God didn't craft only a few world changers. He destined each of us and each of our children to positively impact our spheres of influence, the scale of which is irrelevant. We must be the loudest voice in our children's lives, reminding them that they were crafted in detail by God for greatness. Each of us carries influence somewhere—in the home, in the marketplace, in the schoolyard, or with our best friend or significant other. To live is to influence others.

Sometimes in the parenting journey, we are focused simply on our child's survival, not their positive impact on the world. But we believe each of our children is a little light, a display of God's good nature to the world around them. Let's be sure our expectations for our children aren't merely for them to survive but to thrive as little world changers, bringing light and hope to the people around them. Renowned strengths expert Brent O'Bannon sees people this way:

> I've always believed every human being has their own code for success, their own combination of potential. This combination is not something you search for outside yourself, it's already inside of you. And it's your responsibility to access your potential.[1]

Bailee is a stunning example of a girl who lights up the lives of people around her because she follows God's calling with her talent, passion, and faith. This unfolded through a series of decisions during Bailee's adolescent years. We saw her love for theater on the stage—despite the stage fright—and behind the scenes. She greatly enjoyed preparing actors' costumes, hair, and makeup. She thrived in the arts and specifically in her theater community throughout high school. During Bailee's junior and senior years, we had many conversations about her options for the future. One day Bailee told us she had a passion for cosmetology and asked if we could help her go to beauty school.

As we considered Bailee's request to go to cosmetology school, we relied heavily on the practicality of the Five E's to keep our thoughts about what our daughter should do in line with who she truly is. We looked at what really enthused her over the past several years. We remembered how Bailee would arrive early to rehearsals or stay late, *enthusiastically* serving the theater company. The long hours of back-stage work were *easy* for Bailee. She was known for her ability to do makeup and help her peers look their very best for their parts. Her *excellence* was validated again and again by others. She would come home *energized* and full of joy. She would describe in detail all she had done for the production, and even though she had to wake up early and stay late for each show, the *enjoyment* she experienced as she watched each performance display her handi-work gave her immense satisfaction. The Five E's were evident in Bailee's pursuits. With clar-ity and ease, we sent our girl to beauty school and invested in her future as an artist and styl-ist. O'Bannon goes on to say,

> The way to access your potential is via your talents, your natural patterns of thinking, feeling and behaving. When you identify your top strengths and begin to understand how these strengths apply to your personal and professional life, this knowledge will unlock your potential.[2]

The Impact of One Life

Bailee has experienced tremendous success in her field. After just a few years, she was priv-ileged to learn under a successful salon owner and hair stylist, receiving frequent praise for her natural talent and ever-growing skill. Bailee has developed a strong and loyal clientele at the salon where she works. She has applied her servant-hearted nature in caring for peo-ple's outward beauty *and* ministering to their inward souls. She has learned to listen, offer sound advice, and express care and concern for others while they sit in her chair.

"Once I began my career in hairdressing, the power of understanding strengths really clicked. I work with many different clients, each with their own background, needs, and personality. I've learned how to use my strengths to improve my communication and advance my career. And this has helped my marriage too because I better understand my husband and recognized the different ways we think about things and process them."

—BAILEE (25)

All of us have just one life to live. Each life is like a pebble thrown into a pond. The ripple effect created by the splash of the pebble represents the impact of our lives. For better or worse, our lives will change our pond. Bailee chose to lean into God's call to communicate the beauty of his goodness. From behind her salon chair, Bailee engages her clients, listens to them, and demonstrates her care and concern for them. She creates beauty with her hands as well as with her voice.

Bailee eventually made her way back to the stage—not to help produce plays but to lead people in worship. Alongside her husband, Jordan, Bailee brings her passion for worship and her talent of singing to lead the church into the presence of God each Sunday. Bailee's choices to pursue her strengths and follow her passions have led her to a place of fulfillment and significance, both in the workplace and in ministry. Excuse our bias, but isn't she just a brilliant example of a young woman who cultivated and leveraged her talents into strengths that positively impact the world around her?

Their Way with God

As the oldest of our children, Bailee often takes up the maternal mantle with her siblings. As a shy girl, Bailee could have been the kid who faded into the background, losing herself in the noise and activity of the family. Instead, despite some hard days, she displayed grit and focus as she fought against the temptation to compare. She has become her own best self.

We are so proud of the example our oldest daughter is to her younger siblings. Through her own experience, she has learned the value of calling out and encouraging the talents she observes in the younger siblings. She and Jordan host sibling sleepovers at their place and use their influence to build up the young ones and remind them of their uniqueness and value.

Bailee's ripple effect is magnified in our own family, and as parents, we lean back and watch with such gratitude. She has a similar impact on her friends. She is known as the nurturer among her and Jordan's tribe and is always on the lookout, noticing when others are facing difficult challenges and needing encouragement.

When we learn to move past a focus on who we're not, choosing instead to build on who we naturally are, we allow ourselves to be the very best we can be and engage others to be their best as well. "Train up a child in the way he should go, and when he is old he will not depart from it" (Proverbs 22:6 NKJV). This Scripture indicates there is a way for our child to go, and it's the way God designed for them. We parents are responsible for instilling confidence in our kids and encouraging them to boldly go where they are destined to impact the world for good. As the Holy Spirit gives us eyes to see our children the way God does, we are equipped with wisdom to guide them onto their best path.

Kingdom Seekers

So often the way a child goes will be different from a sibling's path, as we have seen with Ciera and Bailee. But there is one way that is the same for all Jesus-followers. Jesus reminds us, "Seek first his kingdom and his righteousness, and all these things will be given to you as well" (Matthew 6:33).

We have made a priority to instill this kingdom-minded perspective in all our children. It is not optional; it is their DNA as new creations in Christ. Once they have accepted Jesus as their Lord and Savior, our children are unequivocally destined to be kingdom-minded women and men.

As the Holy Spirit gives us eyes to see our children the way God does, we are equipped with wisdom to parent, direct, and guide them onto their best path.

We loved watching Bailee recall the seeds of faith and significance we sowed when she was young. Those seeds anchored her soul in times of indecision, confusion, and struggle. She always could fall back on her relationship with the Lord when her circumstances, her relationships, or her perspective of herself were less than ideal. The world can be mean. It can be very challenging. If we aren't there to point our children toward faith, emphasize their talents, and encourage their strengths, there are plenty of others, including the enemy of their souls, who will line up and tell them what's wrong with them.

One of the paramount roles we play in our children's lives is to anchor them to the truth. We demonstrate and lead them toward a heavenly way of thinking about themselves and a daily, earthly way of experiencing the grace of Jesus at work in their lives. Our children shine when they embrace this truth: "It is for freedom that Christ has set us free. Stand firm, then, and do not let yourselves be burdened again by a yoke of slavery" (Galatians 5:1).

When we empower our kids to become their very best selves, we help them identify and develop their talents and yield them back to the Lord as strengths to benefit the lives of others. This is the point when they experience unparalleled expression, freedom, and fulfillment. Our children cannot thrive in freedom when unfair expectations drive our leadership as parents. Bailee is continuing to develop, and her impact is increasing. But we already see the ripples coming from her life, and that fills us with hope for the rest of our children and reinforces the value of a strengths-based parenting approach, where shining eyes is our standard of success— despite our many admitted failures and missteps along the way.

In the last two chapters of this book, we'll walk you through even more practical, age-specific parenting advice. There is so much to discover and so much to learn! One of our biggest realizations over the years is that the parenting journey has as much growth potential for us as it does for our kids. We learn about human nature, God's nature, and the great impact a life can have when we reinforce our children's strengths and watch them develop a heart to serve.

A Moral of the Tale of Two Sisters

Bailee may never be outgoing like Ciera. Instead, she shines on stage as she leads worship at her church. Ciera may never be the backstage help, yet she continues to powerfully communicate content from stages and podiums, inspiring and challenging those who hear her. This is exactly the way it should be!

Bailee and Ciera are now women in their twenties who are living with shining eyes. They married godly men, and they know who God made them to be. They are confident in their strengths, humble in their expression, and generous in their service to others. Best of all, they are still willing to learn, grow, and develop, and they invite us into their lives as friends as much as parents.

We particularly embrace this declaration that my colleague Maureen Monte, a strengths expert and the author of *Destination Unstoppable*, shares to begin her training and coaching sessions: "I want to make one thing perfectly clear before we begin. I'm not here to fix you, because I don't believe you're broken. I'm here to work with you from a position of abundance...I care about your strengths. I'm here to help you identify your strengths and leverage those talents."[3]

Your children can walk in a full, abundant, and impactful life—regardless of their age. They were made for more than merely living according to their own passions for their own pleasure. There's no better day than today to start calling out the talents in your child and developing the strengths that will change the world.

—————— REVIEW THE PLAY ——————

1. What have you learned about yourself as a parent from this chapter's exploration?

2. What is one way this chapter helped you make a shift toward playing to your child's God-given strengths?

3. What did you discover about your child this week that surprises you or changes the way you interact with them?

4. Which insight or activity from this chapter's Playbook offering is the most helpful to your family right now? Why?

Check out the activities for chapter 6 in the Parenting Playbook on page 185.

Seek *Your* Super

Do not try to be someone else. Strive to be
the person you really are—fully and completely.
This is your best avenue to achieving excellence.

EDWARD "CHIP" ANDERSON

You've probably seen your fair share of Disney movies over the years. If you are like us, you've seen a few of the family favorites multiple times, and the soundtracks play on repeat in your mind. We have decided to embrace this as a good thing because the movie *The Incredibles* happens to illustrate the heart of this chapter.

The movie depicts Mr. Incredible, an insurance salesman, working a nine-to-five job and clearly not living up to his potential or doing something that brings him joy. He is disengaged, moody, and unhappy at home because he is living a dualistic life. He has superpowers but was required to suppress them when he was relocated to live undercover as a normal human being.

Can you relate to Mr. Incredible? Do you sometimes feel as if you've been forced to live a life that suppresses your superpower?

Eventually he can't suppress his identity and strength any longer, and he begins to moonlight as a crime fighter with his best friend, Lucius, also known as Frozone. They often stay up all night listening to police scanners and using their superpowers to counter crime.

These characters gain tremendous energy, fulfillment, and joy from their undercover work.

This is what will happen for us too. Joy happens when we stop getting by and start boldly developing our strengths. Nobody is keeping you from living out your strengths—God certainly isn't. He made those strengths and wants to see you put them into action for yourself, your family, and your community.

Joy happens when we stop getting by and start boldly developing our strengths.

In the story, each Parr family member has their own form of super. Bob Parr (Mr. Incredible) has superhuman strength and durability. His wife, Helen Parr (Elastigirl), is a resourceful and dexterous superhero. Dashiell Robert Parr (Dash) can move at great speeds. His sister, Violet Parr (Vi), can produce force fields and render herself invisible. Lastly, Jack-Jack is the baby in the Parr family. His primary power is shapeshifting, but he has many other powers as well. Look at all this *super* in one family—yet they are living a mediocre life by suppressing their strengths.

Spoiler alert: Mr. Incredible eventually needs help and has to call on the superpowers of every family member. He must shed light on the strengths of each person. To have a happy ending—and might I add, for good to triumph over evil—this family needs to rise up out of their illusion of ordinariness and step into their extraordinary, shining strengths.

This animated tale offers a few calls to action for every parent. The first: You are to model how to live a fulfilled life using your unique talents every day so you avoid a life of duplicity and disengagement. You are made to be you, not a lesser version of you.

The second: You are to celebrate each person's individual greatness and not settle for mediocrity. Look for their version of super. Shed light on the strengths in your child.

If you, like us, have a passion to raise children with shining eyes, smiling faces, and full hearts, look first in the mirror. Do your eyes shine? Does your face smile? Is your heart full? Here are two questions to ask yourself:

1. Do I allow my daily activities—work, school, chores, bills, and so on—to overshadow my exuberance and joy?

2. Do I allow the realities of life to overshadow my child's exuberance and joy?

The answers might take longer than a brief pause to contemplate. Consider journaling through your responses. Are you like Bob Parr before he starts to moonlight as his true self and exercise his strengths again? Or are you tapping into the heart and spirit God gave you?

This chapter is about awakening to *your* God-given strengths so you can walk in them and parent from them. This awareness allows you to model a strength-focused life for your child, and it will help you be a mightier advocate and encourager for your family members' strengths as well. You'll discover that a family that knows their strengths grows their strengths.

Awareness Leads to Authenticity

For my business, I (Brandon) often speak to a roomful of executives. In each of these sessions, titled "Leading with Strengths," I ask the participants to identify the quintessential quality of effective leaders. The most common answers include vision, communication, competency, empathy, trustworthiness, intelligence, a good work ethic, stamina, people skills, strategic thinking, problem-solving, and financial acumen.

All these qualities are great, but a sincere assessment zeroes in on a quality that trumps them all: self-awareness. The most effective leaders know who they are and who they are not. This knowledge gives a person the confidence and competence to make a significant and lasting difference in other people's lives.

To be effective leaders in our home, we need to be self-aware. Self-awareness is a lifelong pursuit that requires us to abandon the unrealistic expectations we might have for ourselves and truly embrace the strengths God has given us.

The last email Jim Clifton received from Dr. Donald Clifton, his father and the creator of the Clifton StrengthsFinder, was about this very thing.

> Another notion about leaders is that each one needs to know his or her strengths as a carpenter knows the tools in his box or as a physician knows the instruments she has available, and a carpenter does not hammer with a saw. So leaders have different tools (strengths)…but the better she knows how to use them the more effective she is as a leader. It is not so much what strengths they possess as leaders—it is knowing accurately what a person has as strengths…This means a leader needs to know what his tools are and exactly when to use each of them.[1]

Leaders who are not self-aware might suffer from "imposter syndrome," which is experienced by individuals who "maintain a strong belief that they are not intelligent; in fact they are convinced that they have fooled anyone who thinks otherwise."[2] Anyone with imposter syndrome is ineffective in influencing those they intend to lead. "The most common symptoms of [imposter syndrome] are negative self-talk; a need to constantly check and re-check work; shying away from attention in the workplace; and forms of overcompensation like staying late at work or not setting appropriate boundaries around workload."[3]

When parents lead from imposter syndrome, they are less confident and more difficult to follow as leaders and role models. A parent who identifies with this syndrome might set unclear or unrealistic expectations, second-guess instructions, or speak in harsh tones. When leaders believe they are imposters, their followers often leave to look for stronger guidance. In our homes, this reality plays out as our kids pay less and less attention to our advice and seek counsel from other sources. In Ephesians we are told, "Fathers, do not exasperate your children; instead, bring them up in the training and instruction of the Lord" (6:4).

Our kids become exasperated when they cannot trust us. They are no different from us when we are evaluating leadership in our workplaces, churches, community groups, sports teams, and volunteer groups. We want to know if those we choose to follow have our best interests at heart. We want to trust them just as our children want to trust us. It is nearly impossible to trust an imposter. We crave authenticity. So do our children.

Charles Swindoll reminds us, "Each day of our lives we make deposits in the memory banks of our children."[4] To deposit strengths into our children, we need to be strong. To deposit confidence into our children, we must be confident. To deposit trust into our children, we must be trustworthy. And to deposit authenticity into our kids, we must be authentic.

Know and Grow Your Strengths

You've spent time paying attention to your child's strengths. There's a good chance you've already started to notice your own "super" as well. We want to encourage you to delve deeper right now to understand your strengths and parent from them. The next step is to identify a few of those natural abilities you bring to your home and family. In our travels, we meet many people who, sadly, do not really know their strengths and subsequently spend far more time trying to learn to be someone they are not.

We have developed a list of parenting strengths available to you at www.analynbrandon.com in the free resource section. In the Parenting Playbook on page 187, we give you further instructions. As you consider the list of parenting strengths, be cautioned: You will be tempted to lament the strengths you wish you had instead of celebrating the ones you possess. Focusing on your lack will never help you discover and develop your "super"; instead, it will lead you to unfulfillment. So resist that inclination so you can know and grow your strengths and inspire your kids to develop theirs.

Play to Your Strengths

We know firsthand what kind of transformation takes place when we identify and walk in our strengths with conviction. I (Brandon) am so grateful I was introduced in 2003 to the strengths-based approach through the book *Now, Discover Your Strengths* by Dr. Donald Clifton and Marcus Buckingham. I had the opportunity to encourage the organization I worked for to participate in training to shift our development philosophy to a strengths-based approach.

For the first time, I was walking and working in my strengths. Each day I served the organization in this way, I saw significant improvement in communication, collaboration, and outcomes among the teams. I was empowered and energized.

I (Analyn) was amazed by the growth in Brandon. I noticed the difference in his joy and effectiveness as a leader, listener, and partner. What he was learning professionally was clearly changing him as a person, a husband, and a dad. He is our kids' coach in life, and he started using his strengths with even more conviction to guide the children through their decisions. As the focus on strengths became more and more natural, he counseled the kids to understand and play to their God-given talents. This became his superpower, and our family became stronger under his new level of leadership.

Soon both of us were committed to watching for and building up the "super" in one another and in each of our four younger ones. It wasn't long before we also introduced strengths-based living to our three older kids. All our kids noticed the difference in us, and we noticed the confidence in them. This is how it unfolds in the life of a family. When we learn to play to our strengths as individuals, we enhance our entire journey of purpose and of parenting.

I have benefited from embracing my strengths while acknowledging where I'm not as strong. I am an outgoing person. In the checkout line at the grocery store, in an elevator, in a coffee shop, on an airplane, or just out for a walk, I enjoy striking up conversations with people. This strength helped me connect with potential clients and become a successful Realtor.

However, when it came to handling very detailed transactions, I struggled. Early in my career, instead of networking with clients and utilizing my strengths, I was laboring to implement processes to handle the meticulous work. The result? Even with hours invested, I didn't see improvement. I became exhausted because I was trying to turn a weakness into a strength.

One day, I (Brandon) was listening to Analyn joyfully talk about a new client and the ways she could help them achieve their goals. When we switched to the topic of the detail work, her voice and body language reflected her frustration. The contrast was significant. We knew she needed to play to her strengths. After some brainstorming, Analyn decided to hire a transaction coordinator to handle the details of each real estate deal. The result was incredible! With more time to devote to the aspects of her business that really utilized her strengths, Analyn tripled her business in one year.

The business benefited from an energized Momma Miller (as our children and their friends affectionately call her), as have all areas of her life. Everyone is proud of her success at work, and more than a few of us are happy she has more joy and energy to live from her strengths at home. She hosts the *best* gatherings for our special family celebrations. With more time to focus on her natural strengths, Momma Miller aptly models the way to live from a strengths perspective and encourages each of our kids to focus on their "super."

"Recognizing my strengths helped me to better define how I approached my belief system altogether. Knowing how I construct information and receive conviction helps me to process opposing viewpoints and connect with people at the core of who they are, rather than attempting to belittle or sabotage the foundation someone has built their life on."

–JORDAN (BAILEE'S HUSBAND) (27)

What have you been modeling for your family lately? Are you ready to play to your strengths in all parts of your life? Take control of the time you would have spent trying to prop up an area of lack and invest it in living according to your gifts and abilities. Review your personal list of parenting strengths. Walk in them. Live and parent from them. God cannot wait to use the real you—the super you.

Discover Strengths Together

You instinctively know what you enjoy. Think back to your childhood—what did you love? I (Brandon) remember how much I hungered for the competition, challenge, and achievement of playing football. I only get to play with my younger boys these days, but the same hunger to achieve excellence and sustain results are two of my most prevalent strengths. Similarly, our children know which activities they are naturally curious about. The activities that make hours feel like minutes and leave kids energized rather than depleted will typically reflect passions and strengths.

The core talents that fuel our interest will be consistent throughout our lives. The activities we are passionate about may change over time, but they are helpful in the process of self-discovery. I can track the foundation of my current passions to the seeds that were sown in childhood. The expression looks different, but the passions and talents have always been there.

As much as you need to know your child's
"who" to make parenting decisions, your child
needs to know your "who" to walk in confidence
in the direction you are leading them.

As we mentioned, during our travels, we meet many people living with an identity crisis. They don't know who they are because they are stuck in the shadow of who they were told to be. The days of telling someone who they should be are fading. Only you know what makes you feel strong, and the same goes for your child. Ownership of one's strength comes through self-discovery. So as much as you need to know your child's "who" to make parenting decisions, your child needs to know your "who" to walk in confidence in the direction you are leading them.

The Making of an Incredible Family

Most people spend much of life thinking that only a select few truly special, chosen, or gifted people exist in the world. People might think, "Most of us are just average Joes, content with mediocrity, not expecting particular greatness to emerge from our lives. We hope our kids will lead decent, respectable lives, but let's be real—they aren't all destined to be world changers, right?"

In contrast, we believe that each of us is created by God with a unique hardwiring that serves a need of this world. The *value* of our influence is not determined by its *scope*. Each child born into this world is made to use his or her genius to benefit others. The greatness of one can benefit many. We believe wholeheartedly that when we learn to celebrate different talents, everyone wins.

Each of us is created by God with a unique
hardwiring that serves a need of this world.

John Buchan—historian, author, and Canada's fifteenth governor general—is credited for saying, "The task of leadership is not to put greatness into people, but to elicit it, for the greatness is there already." Understanding that parents are leaders, this profound statement provides us another call to action—to elicit the greatness that already exists in the child of God placed in our care.

We encourage you to take time each day to consider your child's uniqueness and call out the innate raw talent—the "super"—you see percolating. Share it with them and encourage more of it. If you have kids in high school or junior high, it's not too late. If your children are in grade school, now is the perfect time to introduce them to the concept of mining the greatness within them. You can even begin spotting talents in infants and toddlers. In chapters 12 and 13, we provide more helps to accomplish this.

Our job, our charge, is to raise up children who reflect their heavenly Father and become the men and women they were born to be. By uncovering and living out of your strengths, you are creating a legacy for your children, empowering them to know how to draw from the best in themselves, stay encouraged when they encounter one of their own weaknesses, and ultimately see the best in others. You are not raising an ordinary child; you are encouraging an incredible family in which every person soars in their "super" to influence the people and situations God entrusts to them.

REVIEW THE PLAY

1. What have you learned about yourself as a parent from this chapter's exploration?

2. What is one way this chapter helped you make a shift toward playing to your child's God-given strengths?

3. What did you discover about your child this week that surprises you or changes the way you interact with them?

4. Which insight or activity from this chapter's Playbook offering is the most helpful to your family right now? Why?

Check out the activities for chapter 7 in the Parenting Playbook on page 187.

Don't Buy the Lies

*If you spend your life trying to be good at everything you
eliminate your chances of being great at anything.*

TOM RATH

People ache to be known. It starts at an early age. When your child
looks up at your face to see if you "get" them and appreciate how
special they are, you have a chance to be their mirror. Let your expression and your words reflect the truth about who they are—a person
uniquely and wonderfully made by God.

In discovery mode, we learn who our child is. We can help them
see who they are and which natural abilities and strengths will unleash
their greatest potential.

Just like you, we are in pursuit of truth as our family's foundation.
We have no intention to squander our one chance to parent a child by
chasing lies or half-truths that will derail them and their calling. This
conviction has helped us raise kids who embrace the truth with ease.

Let your expression and your words reflect
the truth about who they are—a person
uniquely and wonderfully made by God.

Our son David is a good swimmer who practices hard and wins many of his races. He has noticed that some kids who excel in this sport have abilities beyond his own. This doesn't faze him because his participation on the swim team allows him to grow in his natural strength—leadership. In his age group, he leads his relay team. On several occasions, his coach has commented on the quality of leadership David brings to the boys on his relay: "They may not be the fastest, but they will be well led and encouraged." This is where and how David shines. He is conscientious, responsible, caring, and excellent at leading others—all qualities we will develop in him as he matures. Best of all, he is comfortable in the truth of who he is—his limitations as well as his strengths.

Countering Lies with Truth

To live in truth and teach from it, we must be informed. We must recognize the lies, particularly those that at first seem harmless but can quickly diminish the impact of your parenting...and a child's life. Unfortunately, some prominent and socially acceptable thoughts are floating around that can do real damage to the development of kids' strengths.

Let's examine and debunk some of these common lies and replace them with new language. You might quickly identify a lie or two you have been holding on to as truth. Know that you're not alone. We've done the same, but now we're working hard to rid our parenting of these lie-influenced practices so we raise kids who are empowered by the truth of who they are.

Lie: Your child can be anything they want if they work hard.

Our society places a high value on hard work. We think effort should equal excellence, all variables aside. Well-meaning friends offered this lie as parenting advice to us. It isn't an easy one to let go of because it sounds so good, doesn't it? But it isn't the truth. Consider this perspective from Tom Rath, a respected researcher and writer on strengths-based leadership:

> There is something you can do better than anyone else in
> the world. You were born with talents as unique as your
> DNA. Yet society keeps telling you that you can be any-
> thing you want to be…if you just try hard enough. This
> age-old aspirational myth does more harm than good.[1]

Some years ago, I met with a business owner who works with ath-
letes to increase their speed and agility. Intrigued, I asked if he ever
worked with kids he couldn't help. He said yes and then told me about
a mom who came in with her daughter, looking for help increasing
the girl's speed and performance on the soccer field. As he trained the
daughter and observed her natural abilities, he realized he probably
couldn't help her reach the level of performance her mother wanted to
see. He tried to communicate this to the mother with no avail. This
scenario begs the question, Could the energy and resources invested in
this young lady's athletic skills have been better spent elsewhere?

We won't know the answer, but we do know that talent affects your
child's ability to perform. We see that clearly in athletics, but it also
applies universally. Don't buy into this lie, wasting your resources and
distracting your child from who they are really meant to be. Hard work
that isn't linked to a talent area will eventually leave your child feeling
burned out, disappointed, and struggling to overcome a low self-concept.

Truth: You can maximize your child's effort by helping them become who they already are.

If your goal is to raise a child whose eyes shine as they experience
and build on their successes, then guide them to apply the bulk of their
effort in their areas of talent. When your child operates from a place
of strength, you will see their self-confidence, joy, and expertise soar in
that area. Rath presents a strong point:

> While people overcome adversity and are remarkably resil-
> ient, the most potential for growth and development lies
> in the areas where you have natural talent to start with. The
> more time you spend building on who you already are, the
> faster you will grow.[2]

The first step in applying this truth is to understand that kids engage more when their activities align with their natural talent.

In many 34 Strong workshops, we demonstrate this truth through a simple activity. We invite people to participate in a simple exercise that will help them improve an area of weakness. Then we ask them to write their names—first, middle, and last—five times in their best cursive *using their nondominant hand.* We give them 30 seconds to write and usually hear gasps, groans, or collective laughter. Interestingly, some adults set their pens down. Knowing how difficult this task is, they don't even try. Others work feverishly to write their name five times using their nondominant hand.

After 30 seconds, we ask them about the experience. Most comment that it was very frustrating. We then ask them to repeat the exercise with the pen in their naturally dominant hand. After we say go for this second round, the room usually falls silent as people engage. We hear pens dropping as the entire class completes the task successfully.

When we ask them to describe the difference, everyone says the second time required much less effort, felt natural, and was so easy that they could even mentally multitask while completing the task. This leads to a great discussion about the link between engagement and our ability to flow in an activity. Flow is the result of doing something continuously, eventually having acute clarity and focus—commonly called being "in the zone."

As a parent, you can position your children to go through life in one of two ways: by (metaphorically) using their weaker hand with enormous effort just to survive or by using their dominant hand and thriving!

Most of us don't use those terms when we talk to our kids, but we often make decisions and give advice that is contrary to what we truly want to see in them. We ache for their eyes to light up. We love seeing our kids "in the zone." We want them to thrive. So let's stop telling them they can be anything they want if they just work hard enough, because when they fail or end up barely getting by, what happens to their self-concept? They become convinced they didn't work hard enough—that *they are not enough* to succeed.

Nothing is wrong with your child. On the contrary, your child is exactly who they were designed to be. Each of us has God-given talents we can leverage to be great.

What does Rath mean on a practical level when he writes, "The more time you spend building on who you already are, the faster you will grow"? He is pointing out that the traits you noticed in your child as a toddler haven't changed. The fiercely competitive child will grow to become a competitive adult. The organized and process-oriented kid will grow to be an adult who thrives with structure and systems. The tenderhearted little one who cares for ailing stuffed animals and baby dolls will grow to be a nurturing adult. Your children don't grow out of who they are; they become more of who they already are.

Lie: You need to raise well-rounded kids who can do most things well.

We often see kids (and parents) crushed under the pressure to be able to do most things well. Parents who embrace this second lie feel it's necessary to register their child for several sports, creative endeavors, and honors classes while also requiring the child to be the perfect sibling, daughter/son, youth group member, and so on. This lie does so much damage to parents and children alike.

Fear can weigh on our children when they believe that not being successful in every area means they won't get into the right school, find the right spouse, earn enough money, or receive awards that positively define their identities.

We aren't saying parents shouldn't expose their children to various opportunities. They should—that's a fantastic way to observe and identify kids' emerging strengths. Rather, we are underscoring the harmful lie that a well-rounded skill set is the only way to a successful, profitable, and happy future for any child.

Most of us think having a well-rounded kid makes us look like great parents. Surely, others can see that we're clearly doing something right as parents when our child thrives in multiple areas. But the truth is, we will miss the mark of being great parents when we are deceived and distracted from identifying who our child is and who they are meant to be.

Truth: When you stop trying to make your kids good at everything, you can start developing their greatness.

We want to help our kids do well at whatever they put their hands, heads, or hearts to. But are we missing the chance to zoom in on their greatness? Are we pointing them in a direction where we found our own success? Do we want them to be like us—or perhaps to be better than we were—by providing more opportunities?

Whatever might motivate us to direct our kids to a buffet of options, in the end, by striving to become well rounded, many children end up exhausted, discouraged, and aimless. How do we steer away from this and build up a child's true strengths? We start with their natural talents and inclinations. We help them put time and effort into developing their abilities and deepening their understanding of their areas of talent. And we encourage them as we notice strengths emerging and becoming honed and applied in several areas of a child's life. In his book *StrengthsFinder 2.0*, Rath presents this helpful formula:

	Talent	(a natural way of thinking, feeling, or behaving)
×	**Investment**	(learning, practicing, developing)
=	**Strength**	(the ability to consistently provide near-perfect performance)[3]

Let's help our kids invest their time and energy in areas where they *can* become great because of who they are. Why strive for mediocrity across the board for the sake of well roundedness?

• • •

Our daughter Michaela is driven and could likely do well at a lot of things, but we didn't buy into the lie that more is better. We stayed in discovery mode with her through the years and have made some intentional and, at times, alternative choices for her personal development and education based on the strengths we see her exhibit.

As a little girl, Michaela enjoyed neatly setting out her clothes every night for school. Later, she took an interest in teaching her three younger siblings how to do the same. Michaela was the daughter who would go into the kitchen unasked and rearrange our spice cabinet because she saw a more efficient way. As she grew older and was responsible for cleaning her room, she did so with great deliberation and order. Her space needed to be decorated just so.

When her sister moved out and she got her own room, Michaela asked for a specific arrangement of furniture and decor. We delayed our response for a couple of weeks because we honestly thought she should just be content with her new real estate as it was. But as we saw her mood and behavior decline, it became clear that the lack of flow and order was having a negative effect on her.

That weekend, we found ourselves in the aisles of a large home store, looking for decorations and organizing systems with Michaela. She had us hunting for accent pieces that would "pop" as she carefully chose just the right shelving and organizing units she envisioned for the space. We headed home and spent the rest of the evening painting, assembling, and hanging all the items she had chosen. Afterward, we saw our little girl exhale in satisfaction as she finally had her space organized just the way she needed it.

This moment wasn't about indulging a spoiled child's whims; it was about allowing Michaela to thrive in her space according to how she is uniquely wired. She thrives with structure, and without a doubt, her organizational talent will play out in her life.

This ability has proven to be both a strength and a struggle—as is natural for all of us—because it affects her schoolwork and how she interacts with teachers. Michaela had trouble transitioning from a small elementary school into a large junior high school, where the social interactions were vastly different. We saw her struggling when she couldn't control the variables as much. We even saw her grades decline.

Realizing she might do better if she had some control over her schedule, we made the decision to transfer her into an independent study, homeschool situation. She is now able to set her own schedule, interact with her certified teachers, and work according to her process on her subjects. Her grades have improved dramatically. We learned to provide opportunities for her to develop her innate talents while also guiding her so she can leverage them productively and successfully.

The shift to an independent format also has given Michaela time to mature in how she uses her strengths when uncontrollable variables arise. She will transition back to the school setting for high school because we feel she will do better in the public arena when she is a little bit older. As Michaela comes into her own and sees how her talents will express themselves in her daily life, we believe she'll be able to strategically apply her gifts to benefit herself and others more effectively. Rather than investing effort into making Michaela well rounded, we are helping her develop greatness by focusing on her abilities and passion for decorating in these formative years.

Lie: If you want to grow, focus on fixing your weaknesses.

Do you remember the report card example I shared in chapter 3? Did you focus on the C? If so, you and the people who attend my seminars are among the majority. When we do this, we leap over the opportunity to discuss and develop the areas where a child is exhibiting a strength, and we miss the chance to honor and celebrate our kids' best efforts. After a child reveals a report card, the conversation at the dinner table should center on their strengths and abilities. Yes, set aside time to tend to areas in which a child needs help or educational coaching, but first, invest comments, time, and energy toward nurturing areas of natural strength in your son or daughter.

> After a child reveals a report card, the conversation at the dinner table should center on their strengths and abilities.

Sadly, many people focus on the greatest weaknesses they see in themselves or others. People are trapped in the lie that they must fix what's wrong with them, and they bring that lie into their parenting approach. This obsession with fixing weaknesses is especially evident during report card conversations with students and performance evaluations with employees. People often walk away from these conversations with downcast eyes, having been reminded of their areas of weakness and their failure to meet certain expectations.

What if we turned such scenarios upside down and focused on a child's strengths or an employee's positive contributions? What if they walked away with confident, shining eyes, having been reminded of the areas where they naturally excel? What difference would that make in the students' and employees' performance and engagement levels? When we focus on weaknesses, people lose confidence. Applying energy and enthusiasm into areas where a person is not naturally talented frequently leads to a poor self-concept and high self-judgment. This is true for children in all stages of development.

Truth: We overcome weaknesses by focusing on strengths.

When we spend all our time trying to fix our deficiencies, we quickly run out of hours in the day. It is enough to give our best effort to the activities in front of us and discover our strengths. Soon we understand that reinforcing our strengths and celebrating our unique purpose is the way to go.

Author, speaker, and researcher Marcus Buckingham offers great insight on how society has oversimplified the definitions of "strength" and "weakness." He explains that people generally understand that strengths are what you are good at doing and weaknesses are what you are bad at doing. Unfortunately, this definition is incomplete. He says instead, "The simplest and most useful definition of a strength is this: Your strengths are those activities that make you feel strong. (The flip side is also true: 'An activity that makes you feel weak' is the best definition of a weakness.)"[4]

When you pour all your energy, skill, and passion into an activity and come home physically exhausted but feeling charged—that is evidence of a strength. For Michaela, our evening spent moving heavy furniture, painting, and organizing may have left her physically tired, but emotionally, she felt magnificent.

"At a young age, whether I engaged in an argument or a soccer game, I always had to win and would usually do whatever it took to win. As I got older, focusing on my strengths helped me realize why I would cry after soccer games if we lost but my teammates didn't seem to care. My competitive nature is a strength—I just have to understand how to apply it."

—MICHAELA (15)

She applied her best effort into her natural talent and evolving passion, and her sleepy eyes were shining. (My eyes were just tired after all that.) The opposite is likewise true. When you are completely drained, empty, and discouraged after a tough activity you hate doing, this indicates a weakness. The synergy between competency and interest reveals a strength.

Buckingham believes that if we can spend 75 percent of our time doing activities that make us feel strong, we can manage the 25 percent of our time taking care of things that make us feel weak. This is how successful people manage their time, and it's how we can direct our children's time. If we help our kids invest the majority of their time doing what makes them feel strong, their confidence and competence will increase, and they will be less likely to despair because of their weaknesses as they compare themselves to peers.

Focusing on strengths doesn't mean ignoring our children's weaknesses or deficiencies; instead, we overcome them so our children are free to explore and develop their areas of natural talent. In our home, we work to help our kids gain a level of competence in areas that could otherwise hold them back from freely pursuing their passions. But we put exponentially more effort into nurturing our kids' strengths because that's where we will see their eyes shine and their engagement level soar.

For example, our youngest son, Daniel, excels in athletics. He joined a flag football team and was one of the best on the squad, earning recognition from his coach as the most valuable player. At the same time, Daniel has a challenge in school: His reading comprehension is below standard. We acknowledge his struggle, and we are working to help him improve. However, instead of spending the bulk of Daniel's time each day working on his weakness, we have taken the approach of applying the 75:25 ratio that Buckingham describes. Each school night, we ask Daniel to give us 15 minutes of focused effort to improve his reading comprehension and 15 minutes focusing on spelling. In return, he is given 90 minutes to play to his strengths by going outside and playing ball or engaging in another activity that energizes and delights him.

Through this process of honoring his built-in abilities, Daniel is making strides in reading and spelling. He no longer views reading as a prison sentence; he sees it as a task to complete so he can then do what he really enjoys.

And boy, does he enjoy performing! Recently, Daniel was practicing his dancing in front of a living room window, and we decided to video him. With his permission, Analyn posted the dance video to social media, and within an hour, we had hundreds of views. By the next day, we had more than 1,000 views of the video. Daniel was delighted to know how many people commented on his talent because he invests effort and energy into it.

When children are defined by their weaknesses, they feel shame and lose confidence. Daniel exhibited this when we focused on his area of weakness. Conversely, when our children are defined by their strengths, they experience productivity and fulfillment. Today, our son is thriving in his strengths and overcoming his weakness.

• • •

Every child will eventually have opportunities to use their strengths to influence far more people than just their families and their immediate circles. Around the corner is college, vocational training, the military, or maybe a career path. Kids whose strengths have been encouraged and supported will play their part with skill, pride, and a sense of duty and honor. Those children-turned-adults will do well as they maneuver life independently *and* as part of communities and teams.

In the next chapter, we will provide four strategies for overcoming areas of weakness while valuing and preserving natural strengths.

─────────────── **REVIEW THE PLAY** ───────────────

1. What have you learned about yourself as a parent from this chapter's exploration?

2. What is one way this chapter helped you make a shift toward playing to your child's God-given strengths?

3. What did you discover about your child this week that surprises you or changes the way you interact with them?

4. Which insight or activity from this chapter's Playbook offering is the most helpful to your family right now? Why?

Check out the activities for chapter 8 in the Parenting Playbook on page 189.

Overcome Weaknesses

*Deep down, our single greatest fear is to live a life of insignificance,
to come to the end of our life and feel like we never really
did anything that mattered. That is our greatest fear.*

DAVE FERGUSON

In his book *Soar with Your Strengths*, the father of strengths-based psychology, Dr. Donald O. Clifton, estimates that for every strength we possess, we have thousands of non-strengths. Therefore, he concludes, we are better off to double down on our strengths and manage our weaknesses.

Clifton illustrates this with a story about the 1984 Chinese Olympic gold medal table tennis team. When the coach was asked about his team's regimen, he shared that they each practiced for eight hours a day on perfecting their *strengths*. When pressed to elaborate, he used the example of the best player on the team, who was known for not having a strong backhand. The coach had him practice eight hours a day on his forehand. His forehand was so strong, it overcame his comparatively weaker backhand, and no player could beat him.[1] When we keep building our strengths, we can often overpower the weaknesses.

Stop Fixing and Start Overcoming

In this chapter, we will share four strategies to help you and your child overcome weaknesses. Keep in mind that a lot of us grew up with the mindset that we needed to fix our weaknesses. When we play to the strengths of a child, however, we don't struggle to *fix* the weakness or change our child into someone they are not. Instead, we reframe our approach to weaknesses.

A great example of this is found in the story of Daymond John, the successful businessman, founder of FUBU apparel company, and member of the long-standing entrepreneur financing show *Shark Tank*. He is very open about his journey to overcome his weakness of dyslexia. As a kid in elementary school in Queens, New York, John excelled in math and science but did not excel in anything requiring extensive reading and writing. He knew he was different. He was eventually diagnosed with a general learning disability, but there wasn't a lot of information on dyslexia, so that specific hurdle wasn't identified.

But a mother knows! In Daymond's formative years, his mom found ways to help him overcome this unnamed weakness. When she had trouble connecting with Daymond about his day at school, her solution was to have an unfinished puzzle sitting on the dining room table, ready and waiting for him when he got home. The task of completing a puzzle brought focus to Daymond and allowed the two of them to discuss the day with ease.

Next, his mother would ask Daymond to read the *New York Times* to her out loud while she cooked dinner, telling him she didn't have time to read the paper during the day and needed to keep up on the news. Again, her creative idea empowered Daymond to learn in a different manner as she encouraged him to be *his* best.[2]

> "I have been placed in leadership roles for a long time, voluntarily and involuntarily. But the typical leadership strengths of influencing and strategizing are where I am weakest. However, I have learned to lead from within groups because I am relational. I build strong, lasting relationships, which I believe makes me stand out as a leader."
>
> –CHRISTINE (LANCE'S WIFE) (24)

Later, Daymond came up with his own solution at Bayside High School. He enrolled in the business co-op program, where he spent alternating weeks in the classroom and at the First Boston investment bank in Manhattan. He discovered his passion in business, where he could use his love of numbers to create something. He founded FUBU in 1992, and as he developed as an entrepreneur, he discovered that he still dealt with reading and writing difficulties, yet his mind was highly visual. He told one interviewer that he maps business plans in his head.[3]

Daymond John was on a journey of discovery—and many of us are too. His mother's engagement likely played a vital role in his development into a successful entrepreneur. She supported his pursuits in many ways, but perhaps her greatest gift to him was her fascination with his mind and strengths. She helped unlock his ability to visualize, build, and create—strengths that allowed him to overcome weaknesses and turn a clothing idea into a passion and success.

Four Strategies to Overcome Weakness

As you embark on this journey, allow yourself to be enthralled with the dreams, ideas, and brainstorming sessions you will have with your young ones and teenagers alike. Discuss what can be done today to get one step closer to seeing the desire, dream, or goal come to pass. Our hope is that you are empowered and released to dig deep with your child to know them as Christ does and to pray for guidance as you lead them toward adulthood.

As you become aware of a child's challenges, you can turn them into assets. In your children's formative years, you can provide them a tremendous blessing by helping them form their understanding of who they are. You have a special opportunity to shape your children's view of themselves, and I encourage you to seize it before someone else does.

Strategy Number 1: Stop It

This strategy seems straightforward enough: If you are not strong at an activity, and it is not necessary for you to continue the activity, stop. If you are an amazing homemaker, you love to entertain your children and their friends, you throw the best parties for your kids, and you make the best goodies, then by all means, keep doing these things. But if you are not strong at picking out the cutest outfits for your kids or don't do well playing board games, then perhaps this strategy applies to you. Ask yourself, "If I were to stop doing this activity, would anyone miss it?"

Why is it sometimes so hard to stop activities we don't enjoy? In a word, conformity. We have been fed an image of what it means to be responsible parents. We hold similar thoughts for our kids. When we look around and see what others can do, we start to play the comparison game, and this leads us to engage in activities that do not make us feel strong and deplete our energy.

This plays out in our kids' extracurricular activities. If your son loves to play the piano but does not seem to engage in soccer, well, there you have it. Double down on piano and just consider another way for him to exercise and engage with a team. If your daughter loves to play sports but you had dreams of her following your footsteps in dance, let her play. When we hold our kids hostage to activities they don't enjoy or excel in, we reinforce the weakness-fixing mentality and truly disengage our children.

Remember this: Time is the great equalizer of us all. We have only enough time to engage in a limited number of activities. The path of strengths will always lead to the greatest return on investment for your time.

Strategy Number 2: Sub It Out

As business owners, we have strengths in two key areas: building networks of trusted colleagues and acquiring new business through marketing and sales efforts. Interestingly, neither of us is strong in accounting. Early in the life of our companies, we tried our best to impersonate bookkeepers. We would set aside time to balance the accounts, reconcile the checkbook, pay the bills...all the things a responsible business owner needs to consider. At crucial points in both of our businesses (though not exactly at the same time), we decided to outsource our accounting.

For 34 Strong, we decided to use a well-researched accounting method and hired a bookkeeper to handle our needs. This decision led to immediate growth of the company. Resources could be reallocated to areas of strength. The key performance indicators quickly began to show an increase in client acquisition and net profit. A businessperson can't simply ignore the accounting work, just as a parent can't stop taking kids to the dentist or providing lunches for school. We need to consider the aspects of our parenting we can sub out so we can focus on our areas of strength.

In chapter 3, we mention Madeline's challenges with math. We sat with her and helped her with the problems, yet this was often frustrating for her and for us. As she matured, we realized she would receive much more from a trusted tutor during a one-hour session than she would sitting with us for two or more hours. Thankfully, our school system provided a resource we could use for this service, and we happily subbed out the math tutoring responsibilities. With the reclaimed time, we were able to engage Madeline and Michaela in leadership roles in the youth ministry we lead. Gaining time back is the key takeaway for subbing things out.

So why is subbing out hard to do? Some of us take great pride in doing things for ourselves, and we pass this belief down to our children. Perhaps you can relate to those who have a hard time asking for help or who believe needing help is a sign of weakness. But consider this: If you plod along in tasks that don't make you feel strong, deplete your energy, and rob you of joy, is that not the essence of weakness?

Which is better, to humble ourselves and ask for help or to continue spending precious resources engaging in tasks that take from us and do not give back? This is an important perspective to instill in our children while they are young. We can reframe one person's area of weakness as an opportunity for someone else to shine in their strengths.

Strategy Number 3: Sync Up

To sync up is to partner with someone who can help you overcome areas of weakness. When our older kids were teens, we would often see them syncing up with other students to work on assignments and complete projects. We enjoyed watching our kids play to the strengths of their peers after they observed those natural abilities in each partner and assigned work accordingly.

Think about the people in your life. Recognize how you sync up with the adults who influence your children all the time. Their teachers, pastors, doctors, dentists, counselors, coaches, and instructors all partner with you as a parent. Sometimes you might forget these relationships are truly an extension of your parenting. They deserve and require your attention and nurturing.

We would all do well to recognize we are partners with these volunteers and professionals for the greater good of our kids. The best partnerships are those in which we assume the best of our partner and recognize them for the valuable contribution they bring to the table. It's remarkably beneficial for our children to see us model positive interactions with all the influencers in their lives.

To sync up successfully requires an admission that another person is more talented, experienced, and trained in an area than we are. The risk sometimes is to infer we know best, especially when it comes to our kids. It is helpful to pause in these moments and regain perspective so that any discourse is led with positive intent for the blessing and benefit of all parties involved.

It's remarkably beneficial for our children to see us model positive interactions with all the influencers in their lives.

Strategy Number 4: Support

Technology is a wonderful tool. Where would we be without our mobile phones, email, text messages, social media, and the other advancements we enjoy? Twenty years from now, this list will seem obsolete, and in fifty years, many items may be forgotten (rotary phone, anyone?). When it comes to overcoming weakness with tools, our daughter Ciera provides an excellent example. She, like Daymond John, had a tough time with certain subjects in school. As she entered high school, spelling was not a strength. Programs that check spelling became Ciera's best support through honors and AP classes in high school and college.

Having the right tools for the right task is a powerful way to overcome a weakness. Whether we rely on our phone's advanced calendar system or post inquiries on social media to find the best plumber, our pursuit of the right support is a sign of strength and should be a lesson we teach our children while they are young. Personally, when we travel with our children, we take advantage of the opportunity to train them to use mapping technology, read a map, and if necessary, ask for directions. Out of seven kids, we know a few of them could be directionally challenged!

Some of the most important support any of us can receive will come from a network of trusted advisors. We operate from the perspective that every successful organization has a board to advise its course and direction and to weigh in on important decisions. As such, we use our close friends and family members as a pseudo board to help us see the pathways and potential problems ahead. We encouraged our kids moving into their adult years to seek counsel from trusted sources outside our family. We know instinctively and from experience that there is…

only so much we know,

so much more we know we don't know,

and much, much more that we don't know we don't know.

These blind spots require illumination from others. Think of this as the flashlight in our dark spaces. Building an alliance of trusted advisors is a skill we hope to instill in our kids.

Family Reinforcements

As we mentioned in chapter 8, we have become increasingly aware that our youngest son, Daniel, struggles with his studies, especially reading. His teacher agrees his comprehension is strong and he's a good student, but his reading struggle is now reflected in his grades. Because our son is competitive and doesn't like to have any weakness, we've had many pep talks with him.

One day, it occurred to us to bring our daughter Ciera into the conversation. She had to overcome similar weaknesses, so she understood Daniel's needs and had advice and encouragement to offer. During a phone chat with her brother, she enthusiastically shared that despite still not having a strength in spelling, she is able to follow her dreams because she follows her strengths. She listed the things she's good at: public speaking, working with people, using memorization as a tool and strategy, and employing technology to make up for weaker areas. She gave Daniel advice to do his best, focus on his strengths, and not worry if he gets behind the other kids because he has other super strengths.

This feedback reinforced our perspective to have our kids focus on their strengths and overcome their weaknesses. Building strengths is not about achieving popularity; it's about discovering what makes a kid shine from within.

"Staying Interviews"

Have you ever been through an exit interview? Many organizations conduct these surveys to study why an associate has decided to leave a company and to consider whether the organization can learn to amend behavior to prevent future employees from leaving as well. This could be compared to waiting until your child is moving away to college to ask them which aspects of your parenting or the home experience were lacking so you could maybe improve for a younger sibling. The interviews are a good idea, but perhaps the information would be more useful while the associate was still with the organization or the child still lived at home.

Perhaps we can learn from organizations implementing a strengths-based approach to their development philosophy. These forward-thinking organizations do what you might call "staying interviews," regularly surveying their employees to learn why the best employees stay with them and how to build on these organizational strengths.

We can parent this way. Whether in the realms of business, family, or personal success, managing weaknesses starts by focusing on strengths.

Conduct your own version of staying interviews by asking questions, paying attention, and remaining fascinated with your child's abilities so you can build those up and help them overcome weaknesses. Like Daymond John's faithful mom, find simple and meaningful ways to focus on a strength when you notice a weakness. Soon a child's strength will unfold into purpose.

REVIEW THE PLAY

1. What have you learned about yourself as a parent from this chapter's exploration?

2. What is one way this chapter helped you make a shift toward playing to your child's God-given strengths?

3. What did you discover about your child this week that surprises you or changes the way you interact with them?

4. Which insight or activity from this chapter's Playbook offering is the most helpful to your family right now? Why?

Check out the activities for chapter 9 in the Parenting Playbook on page 193.

10

Focus on the Positive

Rejection brings out the worst in people.
Love and acceptance bring out the best.

STORMIE OMARTIAN

When you are striving toward a future goal, do you reference last year's calendar? Do you write down the mistakes you made and use them as your new to-do list? No. You begin where you are and plan ahead to reach the finish line. Looking back would be counterproductive, and building on the same old mistakes would sink your plans in record time.

If we parent our kids by focusing on what went wrong yesterday, we miss out on what they do well today. We potentially miss evidence of their calling. Our children will always have faults, and we might be conditioned to first see those faults and dwell on them. Strengths-based parenting reminds us to refresh and reframe our focus on what is *right* with our child. The minute we do, we start to count the successes as more important than the mistakes.

To hear God's calling for each of our kids, we must keep our hearts and minds open to what the Lord has in store for them. Like us, you will find that remaining in discovery mode at every stage helps avoid prematurely presuming you have figured out a child's calling or ability. The apostle Paul speaks of forgetting what has happened in the past and focusing on what is in front of him in his letter to the Philippian church:

> Not that I have already obtained all this, or have already arrived at my goal, but I press on to take hold of that for which Christ Jesus took hold of me. Brothers and sisters, I do not consider myself yet to have taken hold of it. But one thing I do: Forgetting what is behind and straining toward what is ahead, I press on toward the goal to win the prize for which God has called me heavenward in Christ Jesus (Philippians 3:12-14).

Parents can mistakenly tie a child's identity to what they have or have not done. This is a common parenting trap that can diminish the shine in our eyes as we look upon our kids and consider their futures. Each of our children will fail us in one way or another, and we will fail them. Praise be to God, his calling for our children is not determined by our perfection. Rather, our faith in his promises, obedience to his Word, and humble response to our own failures allow us to witness and support his calling and purpose for each family member.

Another way to think of this would be to consider ourselves as doorkeepers for our kids. We look to open doors of opportunity by providing for their education and experiences. We seek to close the doors to misadventure and false teaching that could lead our children astray. As doorkeepers, we are to look to Jesus to show us which doors he is opening and which ones lead in the wrong direction. This is not easy, but it is crucial. We must proceed with humility.

What Will They Remember?

One of my friends shared, "My mother's words still ring in my ears, even as an adult." What are the words, the identity statements, you want your children to remember you saying throughout their childhood? Are those the words and phrases that come out of your mouth most frequently?

Sometimes even our humor or casual observations can unintentionally reinforce what's wrong with our child rather than reinforcing how they shine. We have shared examples from our journeys with Bailee and Ciera. In those early years of trying to focus on strengths, I (Brandon) had to repeatedly catch myself from calling out different aspects of Bailee's naturally shy demeanor in a way that didn't benefit her or encourage her. Over time and with intentional effort, I have shifted my language to use well-timed words to validate and build up the talents I see even when—especially when—Bailee doubts herself and her strengths. She would tell you today that the encouragement from her family helped her through some occasions when she had to overcome her natural fears and hesitations or become immobilized by them.

Refresh and reframe to focus on what is right.

Meanwhile, Ciera's vivacious nature often felt over the top and larger than life. There were times when we were tempted to pull her down and make her a little more even keeled and, I confess, a little more "normal." But we would remind one another that God gave Ciera a very awesome, outgoing talent that could be lived out in a way that would inspire and not offend people. When Ciera was encouraged to take a risk and to step out, she felt emboldened. She became creative and thrived. She quickly learned lessons along the way because she was enthusiastic about things that came easy for her, and she could see excellence emerge and experience that rush of energy and enjoyment when she succeeded. Teaching and guiding Ciera as she developed her talents was like steering a moving ship, which is vastly easier than moving a ship stalled at the docks by self-doubt and discouragement.

We have to be careful not to follow the example of the fourth-grade teacher we met in chapter 4 who sent home her well-intentioned notes that focused only on students' deficits. The last thing we want to see is our children diminished under the weight of discouragement. All too quickly, our kids can internalize the disappointment, the differences, and the lack they see in themselves and start exhibiting destructive behavior, such as drinking, experimenting with drugs, and cutting, to respond to the insecurity and shame they feel.

Should parents always avoid anything negative? Of course not. Absolutely, bring correction and guidance to your children as you teach them how to treat others, walk with integrity, handle trials, and overcome hardships or failures. We can't pass over the hard conversations, but we can redirect our focus from all that is wrong with our children to all that is right.

Sometimes you'll need to recalibrate your focus at home so you are noticing and celebrating strengths rather than zeroing in on deficits. Each time you do, you'll discover the power of your words, your actions, and your commitment to your child. Most of us know from our own lives how negative words have undermined or wounded us. Now is your opportunity to be sure you are the one immersing your child in godly words that heal and guide them now and as they become adults.

The Good News

To reinforce our focus on the positive, we can turn to Scripture. The Good News will shape our thoughts and guide how we use them to encourage and inspire our kids.

In Philippians 4:8, the apostle Paul tells us, "Finally, brothers and sisters, whatever is true, whatever is noble, whatever is right, whatever is pure, whatever is lovely, whatever is admirable—if anything is excellent or praiseworthy—think about such things." This verse becomes our list of focal points to direct our thoughts about our kids. Are we paying attention to their true and noble actions? What have they done that's right today versus what's wrong? When have they embraced purity? What is lovely and admirable in them? And where do we see excellence and actions or behaviors that are praiseworthy?

This direction from Paul is intended to direct our thinking away from a negative focus and toward what is good and true. Avoid the mental mire of looking at ways to pick your kids apart for their mistakes. Let's set our minds on things above and our God-given purpose to prepare our kids to be godly, responsible leaders and authentic people who know who they are. Our example will instill in them a deeper level of dependence on God along with greater self-confidence and competence. All parents are privileged to collaborate with their children on their journey to the future God has planned for them.

Increasing Positive Interactions

To direct our minds in the way of Philippians 4:8 is to continually train ourselves to be in this position of awareness, readiness, and positivity. We believe this idea is easier to grasp and apply if we look at research that shows the benefit of positive interactions. Scientists have landed on a way of thinking and understanding called the "magic ratio."

Dr. John Gottman, a well-known expert on marriage and relationships, and his colleagues conducted an experiment that explored the positive-to-negative ratios in marriage. They evaluated whether a 5:1 ratio of positive-to-negative interactions during conflict would have a consequence on marriage and, specifically, whether it would impact the divorce rate among newlyweds. After studying hundreds of newlywed couples and trying to understand if they would stay together, over ten years, Dr. Gottman and his team discovered that those who practiced the 5:1 ratio had significantly more potential to stay together. In fact, the researchers were able to predict with 90 percent accuracy which couples would be successful in their marriages and which would end their relationships in divorce.[1]

What can we glean from this practice for parenting? I (Analyn) have a case study showing the positive-to-negative interactions ratio exhibited during one morning with our son David. This is a real-life scorecard we can use with our kids, and we encourage you to try it soon in your home. This example is from a typical morning as David was getting ready for school.

1. We miss the alarm because David and I had been up late finishing a project for school. When we're both in the kitchen, I turn to David and say, "You should have made your lunch the night before. Now we're going to be even later." Score: positive 0; negative 1.

2. We are putting on our coats and gathering our bags when I say in a loud voice, "David, if you kept your room clean, you wouldn't have to search for your coat this morning." We rush around several more minutes until he finds the coat in his room. Score: positive 0; negative 2.

3. We get in the car, and before I back out of the driveway, I notice David has brought the water container I drink from during the workday. On his own initiative, he grabbed it for me when he saw it by the door. In a very expressive way, I share my gratitude with him and say thank you. Score: positive 1; negative 2.

4. During our drive, we realize David has left his sports bag on the kitchen table. With a tone of disappointment, I say to David, "You can be so forgetful sometimes and not appreciate the value of my time." I am frustrated because I know I will have to drop David off at school, go back to the house for the sports bag, and return with it so David will have it for practice. Score: positive 1; negative 3.

5. As we pull up to the school's roundabout, I say my good-byes to David. He stops me for a moment to remind me I have an after-school appointment with his teacher. I tell him this is very nice and helpful because I honestly had already forgotten. I appreciate his reminder. Score: positive 2; negative 3.

This scene doesn't present a shining example, but it certainly presents an authentic one. Change takes a concerted effort and awareness. If we aim for and maintain the 5:1 ratio, David has a significantly greater likelihood of being engaged with our family, being productive in his schoolwork, and being successful in sports.

"I am a strong, relational problem solver, and that has sometimes left me feeling vulnerable when I didn't see eye to eye with someone or I couldn't figure out why someone didn't feel the same way about a situation. However, when I learned how to use my relational abilities, I could understand others as individuals and appreciate how they express themselves differently. It's definitely not always personal— just different."

—BAILEE (25)

We all need positive reinforcement on a regular basis. Why would our kids long for anything less? As parents, we can reinforce this positive 5:1 ratio. Here are some ways to ensure a stronger ratio in day-to-day living:

- Meaningful praise highlights the value of what a person

has done and is specific. When Analyn recognizes David for bringing out the water bottle and being thoughtful and for reminding her about the teacher conference and being helpful, she can be specific in the moment, and she can refer to those examples later.

- Our kids want to know we notice them. They long for us to pay attention to the effort and energy they put into their chores, into being kind to their family and their friends, and into their schoolwork, activities, and athletics. When you recognize what matters to your child and take special care to understand who they are and why it's important, you will hit the bull's-eye.

- Consider this ratio as a starting point! As believers, our hope can be to exceed this and to use our thoughts and first responses to build up our kids and give God glory for every positive interaction and step of progress in a child's life.

- As Don Clifton said, "Individuals are always stronger when they have their success and strengths clearly in mind."[2] Remind your child of their successes and their strengths. More important, remind them that they are loved and valued for being exactly who they are.

Our children need to be reminded of their value, so our praise and encouragement need to be heartfelt. Try writing Philippians 4:8 on a note or on your mirror so you see it every day and seek to start your day with the perspective to see your child through the filter of what's right, what is noble, what is true. Throughout each day, you can ask, "What can I see in them that God sees? What can I see in them that others may not?"

Discipline with Strengths in Mind

What about the situations when we clearly don't see something to praise in our child's behavior, and instead, we know that the child needs to be disciplined? How does our commitment to strengths make room for discipline? The truth is, this approach to parenting can inform the way you discipline and will make those instances more effective in the correction of behavior and more influential for transformation over the long term.

Researcher Dr. Lea Waters illuminates this in her book *The Strength Switch*: "Strengths-based parents still need to discipline their children. The difference is that they approach misbehavior from a constructive, growth-oriented perspective that gives kids a clear idea of the strengths that can be used to change for the better."[3] Strengths-based discipline is grounded in the premise that by nature, we are motivated to self-develop.

If we aim for that "constructive, growth-oriented perspective," we are likely to provide our child with solutions based on their strengths. For example, let's say your daughter repeatedly leaves the back door ajar after putting her bike on the back porch. It has become a safety and security risk for your household. You want to discipline her in a way that maximizes her strengths. She has been absentminded about this habit, but you know she has strong organizational skills. After the last warning about locking the back door is not heeded, you decide your daughter's bike-riding privileges will be taken from her for the week. Instead of riding with her friends for a half hour after school each day, you ask her to create a master responsibility grid so each family member can quickly see what their daily "before bed" tasks are.

Now instead of your daughter repeatedly making a mistake and you repeatedly pointing it out (and messing up that 5:1 ratio!), you have given her a chance to use a strength to create a proactive solution. While completing this task, she also gains a better understanding of each family member's responsibility. That serves as a reminder that the requirements asked of her are not beyond what is asked of each person. There is a great chance that your daughter will take ownership of the list and take pride in improving the family's routine. With "locking the back door" written on her part of the master checklist, she is less likely to forget, and she is more likely to be the one who reminds other family members to finish their priority tasks.

A mistake becomes an opportunity for strengths to be reinforced.

This perspective can make a huge impact on how your child receives correction—not as a disconnected action against them but as a strength-building expression of your care for their growth.

A mistake becomes an opportunity
for strengths to be reinforced.

What You Tell Your Child (Even When You Say Nothing)

On our best parenting days, we watch our words. We eliminate criticism and negativity, get rid of blame, and minimize sarcasm, being aware that our children need to hear positive reinforcement from us. We might not realize that our beliefs about a child and any low expectations we harbor about them will also be communicated. Psychologist Timothy Davis, an instructor at Harvard Medical School, cautions that those thoughts drive what we choose to pay attention to and the heart of our response when we interact with a child.

> If you believe that your kids are lazy, selfish, irresponsible, etc., even if you never call them any of these things, it will have a damaging impact on your positive to negative ratio. What we think influences what we see. If we think our child is lazy, we can't help but selectively notice the times he or she acts in a lazy way and notice fewer of the times that he or she is industrious. What we think about our child also influences how we act. If we think our child is irresponsible, even if we never say so directly, we might subtly express that lack of trust by not giving our child opportunities to be responsible. So, even if you don't verbalize your negative view of your child, the message gets through loud and clear through these subtle cues.[4]

What we decide to turn our minds to again and again will shape us. Our beliefs about each child and their actions and motivations will have a direct impact on how we will treat them; the subtle nuances of our behavior betray our thought process. You are telling your kids what you think about them without even saying a word. Be sure your thoughts are focused on their potential and value.

When we look through the filter of strengths, we notice the areas of a child's greatest potential. Maureen Monte writes, "Identifying and honoring the strengths of others allows them to provide value, perhaps in ways that had not previously been considered."[5] We want to pay attention to each child and notice what they do that's positive. We want to be empathetic, remember that they are growing and learning, and put ourselves in their shoes. We are to be respectful and understand that our children will go through difficult times, they will have emotional outbursts because they are immature, and they are becoming who they are meant to be. It's a process.

> When we look through the filter of strengths, we notice the areas of a child's greatest potential.

If we can maintain a positive view of our child, we can be on their side and stand up for them. When we take disciplinary measures, our child will already know that we are for them and not out to get them. Children receive words of correction and instruction better when they know that we have their back, that we will lead the way, and that we will support them all the way!

Our kids have been given to us as gifts from God. How we see them and treat them—in times of praise and times of correction—reflect on our acknowledgment of that gift.

—————————— **REVIEW THE PLAY** ——————————

1. What have you learned about yourself as a parent from this chapter's exploration?

2. What is one way this chapter helped you make a shift toward playing to your child's God-given strengths?

3. What did you discover about your child this week that surprises you or changes the way you interact with them?

4. Which insight or activity from this chapter's Playbook offering is the most helpful to your family right now? Why?

Check out the activities for chapter 10 in the Parenting Playbook on page 195.

11

Declare the Truth
over Your Children

*Let the little children come to me, and do not hinder them,
for the kingdom of God belongs to such as these.*

JESUS

When we declare truth over our kids, we are declaring what is and what is yet to be. This emboldens them in their strengths and in their faith. We want our kids at every age to believe in who they are and to understand they have been endowed by their Creator with certain gifts, talents, and abilities. Speaking God's truth over our children instills values and morals, and it opens them up to how the Holy Spirit is working in them to take them in the direction they are to go.

In this chapter, we'll explore how you can initiate this practice in your home whether you have a girl or a boy, a toddler or a teen. We can vouch for the power of this particular exercise. Not only does it plant seeds and bear fruit in our children; it grounds us in God's promises and empowers us to parent in his strength.

Speaking God's truth over our children opens
them up to how the Holy Spirit is working in them
to take them in the direction they are to go.

Do I Have What It Takes?

When I (Brandon) first read John Eldredge's book *Wild at Heart*, I was considering what type of man I wanted to become. His questions spoke to the fundamental longing for understanding and identity.

> Deep in a man's heart are some fundamental questions that simply cannot be answered at the kitchen table. Who am I? What am I made of? What am I destined for?…God meant something when he meant man, and if we are to ever find ourselves we must find that. What has he set in the masculine heart? Instead of asking what you think you ought to do to become a better man, I want to ask…*What makes you come alive?* What stirs your heart?[1]

I was asking this as a father, husband, and professional. And while Eldredge posed these key questions in the context of a man's journey, I guarantee that most every father and mother wonder this very thing during many seasons of the parenting experience. We have both gone through times of questioning whether we have what it takes to be great parents. When is the last time you went to bed, turned out the light, and stared into the darkness with this question on your mind and heart: "Do I have what it takes to be a great parent? To do what I am called to do? To make it through the day?"

Our children are asking the questions too.

Over the past several summers, we have watched our youngest son, Daniel, flourish on the local swim team. When Daniel was preparing for the championship meet the summer he was eight years old, he was favored to win gold in every event for his age group. Not only that, but Daniel was on pace to break several league records, some that had stood for more than 25 years.

As Daniel trained for the big event, we could tell the weight of the opportunity was starting to affect him, and we could see he was getting nervous. As part of my strategy to equip my son to do his best, I made a point to speak two truths to him several times a day and before each of his races: "Daniel, you have what it takes!" And "Son, you have the heart of a champion!"

We watched our son shine that year. Not only did he win a gold medal in every event, earning him high point honors for his age group, he also managed to break three long-standing league records and anchor his relay team to break a fourth record.

Each time one of our children faces a new challenge, the question of whether they have what it takes is in their minds and hearts. Every time one of our kids is faced with the peer pressure to go against their moral code to do something just because their friends are doing it, they will wonder, "Do I have what it takes to stand up when the going gets tough or the path is lonely?" It is our job to remind our kids over and over that they do, in fact, have what it takes to live a life from their strengths and their faith.

We are here to encourage you because we've learned how to be strengthened in those moments by declaring truths to ourselves and to our kids. As you bring this practice into your life and home, you'll discover that the answer is a shining yes. God has equipped us to be the best parents we can be! He has uniquely wired each one of us to use our strengths to raise kids empowered by their strengths and their faith to meet life's challenges and overcome life's failures. With God's grace and power at work through our strengths and even in our weaknesses, we most certainly have all we need to stand firm and be resolved in our journeys as powerful parents.

Stand on Scripture

God has uniquely gifted each child in your care with his divine genius to accomplish the mission he has given them. Whether you have one child or five, whether your nest is filled with children who share your genetics or who share your heart through adoption or foster love, this responsibility is real—and really amazing! Nothing is more pivotal for your success than standing on the parenting platform based on Jesus's words, "Seek first his kingdom and his righteousness, and all these things will be given to you as well" (Matthew 6:33).

From the time our kids were very young, we made sure they knew that the most important thing they could become is a man or woman of God. And like all important heart lessons, this one required us to demonstrate it over and over in the life of our family. Our kids know that being a man or woman of God is evident in how we love, serve, and consider others. They have witnessed and participated in the use of God-given talents to benefit and give back to the people around us.

God has uniquely gifted each child in your care with his divine genius to accomplish the mission he has given them.

If you were to ask our 11-year-old son, David, or our adult son, Lance, "More than anything else, what do your parents want you to be when you grow up?" both would respond, "A man of God!"

We believe the call of God for each child will be unmistakable. The prophet Jeremiah gave us this perspective of the calling of God: "If I say, 'I will not mention his word or speak anymore in his name,' his word is in my heart like a fire, a fire shut up in my bones. I am weary of holding it in; indeed, I cannot" (20:9).

Scripture blesses us with powerful insight into how we might parent our children into their purpose and calling. Get ready. We will share how to uplift your child and glorify the Lord by declaring his truths with hope and faith.

Declaring Truth

The idea of declaring truth over a child can sound intimidating. But you have the ultimate resource to draw from. The Bible overflows with God's truths and promises. Introduce a regular habit of praying key Scriptures over your kids, and God's Word will raise your hope and potential—and your child's.

Relying on our strengths-based parenting approach and our Christian values, we believe that biblical truths shape our kids and provide them with insight into how they can draw strength from God and use their strengths for God. To keep verses in focus, I (Analyn) write them on the kitchen chalkboard and change them for seasons and occasions.

Sometimes I post a note right at the front door to reinforce into our kids' hearts and minds what God says over them.

Verse by verse, we are adopting the Father's view of our kids, and we are reminded that they are his and are purposed, valued, transformed, and strengthened in his power. Here we have listed, by category, several of the verses and truth proclamations so you can begin to use them right away. We declare truth over our kids in our prayer time as a couple and when we are with the kids. Gathering a collection of verses becomes a joyful practice.

PURPOSE

"We are God's handiwork, created in Christ Jesus to do good works, which God prepared in advance for us to do" (Ephesians 2:10).

> **Truth to declare:** *God has a purpose and a plan for your life.*

"You are the light of the world. A town built on a hill cannot be hidden" (Matthew 5:14).

> **Truth to declare:** *In God, you are the light of the world.*

"We know that in all things God works for the good of those who love him, who have been called according to his purpose" (Romans 8:28).

> **Truth to declare:** *God will work out his purpose in your life.*

TRANSFORMATION

"If anyone is in Christ, the new creation has come: The old has gone, the new is here!" (2 Corinthians 5:17).

> **Truth to declare:** *You are a new creation in Christ!*

"Then you will know the truth, and the truth will set you free" (John 8:32).

> **Truth to declare:** *You know the truth, and the truth sets you free.*

"It is for freedom that Christ has set us free. Stand firm, then, and do not let yourselves be burdened again by a yoke of slavery" (Galatians 5:1).

> **Truth to declare:** *You are free in Christ—don't be burdened.*

VALUE

"I praise you because I am fearfully and wonderfully made; your works are wonderful, I know that full well" (Psalm 139:14).

> **Truth to declare:** *You are precious and valuable to the Lord. He made you, and he loves you.*

"See what great love the Father has lavished on us, that we should be called children of God! And that is what we are! The reason the world does not know us is that it did not know him" (1 John 3:1).

> **Truth to declare:** *You are a child of God, a part of his family forever!*

"This is love: not that we loved God, but that he loved us and sent his Son as an atoning sacrifice for our sins" (1 John 4:10).

> **Truth to declare:** *God loves you and sent his Son to save you from your sin.*

STRENGTH

"The Spirit God gave us does not make us timid, but
gives us power, love and self-discipline" (2 Timothy 1:7).

> **Truth to declare:** *God has made you*
> *bold, powerful, and self-controlled.*

"Have I not commanded you? Be strong and courageous.
Do not be afraid; do not be discouraged, for the LORD
your God will be with you wherever you go" (Joshua 1:9).

> **Truth to declare:** *You are strong and*
> *courageous because God is with you!*

"I can do all this through him who gives
me strength" (Philippians 4:13).

> **Truth to declare:** *You are strong in*
> *Christ, who gives you strength!*

When Declarations Take Root

Declarations reinforce what we know to be true for our kids, and our hope in these declarations comes to fruition when we hear a child repeat these truths and promises with understanding and personal conviction. There might not be a more rewarding and humbling moment than the first time your child embraces the truth of who they are in Christ.

Recently, our daughter Michaela made a video describing her experience at a youth retreat. In it, she conveys the real journey of a 14-year-old finding her faith. She shares that for some time, she has believed in her relationship with God, but she hadn't yet cherished or valued it. She goes on to share, with great joy, how she had a personal encounter with the Lord at the camp that opened her up to his love for her. It was not through one incident but in the unfolding of truth and awareness over the weekend that she witnessed and felt the grace of her heavenly

Father, the kindness of Jesus, and the power of the Holy Spirit. She is changed. You can see it in her shining eyes as she recounts this shift from head knowledge to heart passion.

"When I joined the swimming team, I thought it was too hard and wanted to quit. But I worked hard and broke records. I used my strengths to be competitive. I really like to win."

—DANIEL (8)

You can bet that we were beaming with pride as we watched this. Then our joy deepened even more as Michaela used this video message to encourage other teenagers to consider their own journey of faith and to discover God as the Maker of the heavens and the earth. In her unique, enthusiastic way, Michaela shared her fears and frustrations and some of her wonderings and wanderings. She even used a couple expletives as her thoughts tumbled into sentences. Her mom and I decided not to hold it against her because we were so pleased with the *important* words our daughter was saying—words of God's truth we had planted in her heart for years.

Her account is not merely the tale of a kid caught up in her camp experience elation; we *see* the transformation in her when she is home. As she walks forward in her faith with new conviction, we will eagerly watch for how her natural strengths line up to serve God and bolster her faith because we believe that when a child's faith in God and her confidence in herself are linked together, she will have impact for eternal purposes.

Truth Emboldens Strengths

Our identity in Christ is our great strength that will guide and inform all our other strengths. So in addition to speaking to our kids about the truths we see in them through the Scriptures, we also declare their strengths.

In chapters 4, 5, and 6, we explored a way to identify a child's shining and secondary strengths by watching for the Five E's of enthusiasm, ease, excellence, energy, and enjoyment. The heart of this book is about identifying strengths and consistently validating and declaring them.

By declaring over your child the strengths God has bestowed on them, you reinforce who they are as a unique, loved child of God. Reinforcing this truth will free them from a lack of confidence, from striving against incompetence, from "fixing" weaknesses, from needing to be who they're not, and from suffering imposter syndrome. Ultimately, it will free them to flourish and serve God and others through their innate gifts.

———————————

Our identity in Christ is our great strength that will guide and inform all our other strengths.

———————————

Stay encouraged as you bring this life-giving practice to your family. The day you see your child freely claiming, owning, and sharing their strengths and attributing them to the Lord is a day you don't want to miss.

—————————— **REVIEW THE PLAY** ——————————

1. What have you learned about yourself as a parent from this chapter's exploration?

2. What is one way this chapter helped you make a shift toward playing to your child's God-given strengths?

3. What did you discover about your child this week that surprises you or changes the way you interact with them?

4. Which insight or activity from this chapter's Playbook offering is the most helpful to your family right now? Why?

Check out the activities for chapter 11 in the Parenting Playbook on page 199.

12

Spot Strengths in
Toddler to Tween Years

*I have no greater joy than to hear that my
children are walking in the truth.*

THE APOSTLE JOHN

As the parents of seven children, we have seen the vast differences between each of the little human beings we have brought into this world. We have walked through the valley of the "terrible twos and threes" as well as the potentially dangerous terrain of the "mean tweens." We have survived, and we continue to watch blessings unfold in our kids in the form of strength, character, faith, and love.

The hope we share comes from experience and from staying engaged and interested in *who* each of our children is and the strengths God has placed in them. We pray we can offer these gifts of insight and empowerment to you as well. You'll discover in this chapter how to spot the strengths in your children from toddler age through the preteen years. Combine that understanding with a renewed fascination with who God made your child to be, and you have a healthy foundation for an intentional, powerful, and spiritually sensitive parenthood experience—and your kids will have this foundation from which to grow and blossom.

Toddler Tug-of-War

In our early years of raising children, we asked ourselves not who our toddlers were but rather what our expectations of them were and what rules and consequences we should establish. Our schedule was regimented, and our discipline was consistent. We hoped this would result in a well-behaved toddler—that was our goal.

Like many parents and our peers at the time, we employed the system of reward and discipline to manage our first batch of toddlers. It was somewhat dizzying—one minute we would dangle a reward in front of a child, and the next minute we would enforce a time-out. This back-and-forth between reward and discipline left us exhausted and sometimes led to unnerving experiences. We look back on those now and can smile because we know those failed attempts had more to do with the toddler's unique nature than with the defiance we believed was being displayed.

A perfect example occurred in a very public place (of course!). I (Analyn) remember it vividly. Ciera was three, and I was pushing her around in a cart at Target while I picked up some household items. She spotted item after item she wanted to add to my shopping list. As we turned down one tempting aisle, she spotted a bright and shiny object she wanted to tote around while we shopped. I gave in to her carrying the item but explained that it was not going home with us. I felt that holding the treasure was a reward for being happy (and a bit of a bribe). You see the disaster in the making, don't you?

As we approached the next available register, I started to load items onto the conveyor belt. I smiled at her and gently took the item out of her hand. She was still beaming, certain that it too was going to ride the magic conveyor, end up in a bag, and go home with us. Instead, I set it off to the side. Oh my. Out of this tiny, cute girl came a blood-curdling scream. In an instant, all eyes were on cash register number seven to witness what I will forever call the Shiny Object Showdown. Ciera kept reaching, and I kept blocking. As the screams escalated, a few concerned citizens probably considered calling child protective services. Not knowing what else to do, I left my cart at the checkout counter and carried my hollering mess of a toddler out of the store. I felt she had "won" that showdown. It pains me that those early years of parenting were characterized by winning and losing.

We want you to know you don't have to live this way. The shift from the battle of wills to the building of skills will bring more peace and better outcomes. But the first step is to stop playing out the tension of "good cop, bad cop" and start playing to their strengths.

Parenting Replay

Dr. Mary Reckmeyer shares that a 23-year longitudinal study of 1,000 children in New Zealand found that a child's personality traits at age 3 show remarkable similarities to his or her personality traits at age 26. This study supports the theory that even individuals' core personality traits, interests, and passions do not change as much as we might think.[1]

The shift from the battle of wills to the building of skills will bring more peace and better outcomes.

Become a student of your child. Learn, watch, ask questions, pay attention to them in different environments, and consider their reactions to adults and to playmates. Note when they are most at peace—when they seem to "go with the flow" or feel most comfortable. Consider keeping a journal of your child's highs and lows to help you identify key factors and triggers.

Speaking of a lesson learned…now that Ciera is 22 and we have shifted toward a strengths-based approach to parenting, I (Analyn) can look back on the Shiny Object Showdown and see my daughter's strength as a factor in her behavior that day. Ciera is a competitive person. Instead of providing a positive outlet for this strength, I inadvertently set up a situation that ended the afternoon with tears and without *anything* on my shopping list.

Let's do a replay of that day, applying strengths-based wisdom. I head into the store already aware of Ciera's trait of persistence and her passion to achieve. Instead of allowing her to grab and carry the shiny object, I turn our shopping errand into a game. I ask her to help me find all the items on the list. To make it more fun and to reduce distractions, I hand her my watch and set a goal of 30 minutes for the two of us to fill the cart and make it to the checkout line.

This structure for our shopping trip would have given her a way to express her talent for achievement and to focus in a constructive way. It would have united us rather than divided us and avoided a "me against you" mindset.

Spotting Talent in Toddlers

As you become aware of your toddler's talents, you will learn to teach them in ways they will best understand. You'll experience the great joy of unearthing the genius in your toddler and watching with amazement and excitement as they grow into who they will become. You can partner with them to develop their strengths and guide them to use talents and abilities to serve God and their unique purpose. We are tasked by God to raise children in the way they should go, and when they are old, they will not turn from it (Proverbs 22:6). Imagine your toddler growing up in an environment in which they are raised this way—with a focus on the way *they* should go.

The Five E's of Strength Identification for Toddlers

Seeing the Five E's of strength identification in toddlers is not quite the same as spotting them in tweens, teens, and young adults. However, if we notice which activities our little ones are drawn to, the talents do become apparent. As a reminder, the Five E's are enthusiasm, ease, excellence, energy, and enjoyment.

Toddlers show signs of enthusiasm when they want to do things repeatedly. Small children's preferences are not a mystery. When we observe, the signs will become clear. When an activity comes easy for toddlers, they show above-average inclination that leads to glimpses of excellence. The energy is evident when they can stick with something beyond their usual attention span, and the enjoyment is clearly expressed when they want to get back to the game, activity, or pursuit whenever they have the opportunity.

One mother we spoke with shared how her daughter would stand at the door of the day care and greet all the children as they came into class. She wasn't taught this behavior; she intuitively wanted to make other children feel welcome. Another mom shared how her three-year-old daughter would watch a children's program and then continue the scene with her baby sister, stuffed animals, and pets. This mother marveled at her daughter's creativity.

Can you think of a time when your toddler showed great interest in an activity or an above-average ability in an area of play?

Our toddlers instinctively follow the path of their greatest talents without instruction. In its early stages, talent does not necessarily equate with skills. It's too early to detect excellence as we usually define it. However, some of our children will show hints of talents that might emerge later as strengths that shine.

When Daniel was a toddler, he constantly played with his blue toy guitar. He would stand in front of the family and boldly strum away on the instrument as though he were leading us in a special song. If a song was playing around him, we marveled how he was able to move his little body to the beat of the song even if the noise from the guitar was not in tune with the music.

"I like to challenge myself physically and mentally. Like using strategy to win a chess game or putting people on my team in position to do their best. I also like helping people with things that might be challenging to them. These are some of my strengths."

—DAVID (11)

Each year, our family goes on a vacation to a resort called Camp Sacramento, where the campers are invited to participate in a variety show. One year, Daniel's siblings and cousins planned to dance to a certain song. When the music began, there was little Daniel on stage with his blue guitar, standing in front of his family members and smiling away as he swayed his body to the music, looking surprisingly coordinated for such a little boy. As Daniel matured into his grade school years, his enthusiasm to perform for the family only increased. He would take great pleasure in creating and performing different dances.

All of the Five E's were visible in Daniel's physical adeptness and performance as a young boy and when he got older. Years later, we could recall his talent for moving his body to the rhythm of music and compare it to his ability to swim different strokes with near flawless ability. At swim meets, every time Daniel races, we see spectators stop what they're doing to watch him do the butterfly or breaststroke.

Allow yourself to become as curious as a little child. Watch your children and learn to know them better as they grow and become more aware of their strengths in grade school.

Searching for Strengths in School-Age Children

Can you remember when you first felt strong? I (Brandon) was in sixth grade, and I had joined the basketball team at my elementary school. I enjoyed playing the sport and being around the guys. I liked honing my skills to be a better basketball player, but what I really enjoyed was the strategy involved. I carefully watched as the coach drew up plays and told each person what their role was and where to go, what to do, and how to succeed. I can remember writing down those plays and then going to my dad's office before practice to make copies of them to pass out to the others. I wasn't asked to do this; I was just intrigued with the idea of helping people be successful in the sport. During the season, I didn't play a lot. When I did, I was okay, but I knew this wasn't going to be an area of great strength.

However, the future coach and strength seeker in me was born. I was fascinated and definitely had all the Five E's firing when I started finding the best players and putting them into the best positions to achieve the best outcomes.

This talent carried over into group assignments at school. I gladly took the lead, positioning the players on the team, so to speak. I loved to see people doing what they did best, and when it was my opportunity to shine, I stepped into my strengths with ease. What an early lesson in my life. Long before I knew that it was healthy to lean into one's strengths and to expand a strength into other arenas, I was experiencing the benefit of that very truth.

Enjoying the Age of Engagement

Parents can enjoy watching children's talents unfold during the school-age years. Dr. Lea Waters describes a parent's role:

> In the phase during early to mid-adolescence, a child becomes clearer about his passions and chooses to more systematically develop particular strengths...Your role is to provide resources in the form of opportunities and relationships to help your kids develop high-level skill in their strengths.[2]

School kids show us the Five E's when and where their levels of engagement increase. When a child makes time for activities, we can see the evidence of their strengths shining through them. Children follow the light. This light is their joy, happiness, and delight in doing the things they love the most. During their tween years, their strengths become easier to identify if we know where to look. When we ask them about their school day, we can notice their enthusiasm as they describe a particular activity or interaction. When they show us their work with an energetic response to a subject or assignment, we're given a glimpse into the excellence that might unfold in time with the right opportunities.

The hope is that by the time our kids are tweens, they know what makes them feel strong and what pursuits are less enjoyable. If they've grown up under a steady diet of negative reinforcement, this is the stage when they could start to become closed and less expressive with their strengths. If this is the case, take heart—there is still time to shift the parenting approach and really dig in with your kids to find the Five E's in their daily tasks.

Strength Identification for Tweens

Looking for the Five E's in the school-age years and particularly in the tween years requires us to engage our kids to help us detect the presence of talent in their school, play, and extracurricular activities. Tweens can and will tell us the story of their strengths if we are willing to listen. We commonly ask our kids whether an activity made them feel strong. This helps us make sure that they are still working through the Five E's and that we are maximizing their resources and ours.

This age group is just entering that awkward prepubescent period of their lives when they naturally become more self-conscious. Helping them remain confident in their strengths is a powerful way to guide them through this season of life and a great way to prepare them for their transition from children into teenagers.

Tweens can and will tell us the story of their strengths if we are willing to listen.

A word of caution here: Activities our tweens might excel at are not necessarily pursuits they will enjoy enough for long-term development. Recently, I (Brandon) spoke with a boy about his piano lessons, and he shared that his parents required him to take piano. Even though he was a strong player, he really didn't enjoy the practice—and certainly not the recitals.

Parents commonly confuse good performance with strengths. When our kids' eyes stop shining, it's time to step back and ask ourselves and our child whether this is an activity worth the investment of time and energy. I have coached many adults who were essentially forced to play sports or an instrument or pursue a specific education to satisfy their parents' demands, only to abandon the activity later in life with some resentment.

There will also be situations when one part of an activity sparks a child's shining eyes, but the full experience doesn't. My basketball experience is a perfect example. I really did like basketball, but it would only take someone asking a few attentive questions to discover that the observing, planning, strategizing, and leading opportunities were far more exciting and energizing for me than playing the sport ever was. That's why the questions are important in our communication with our kids.

When Something Is Missing

We can help our tweens maneuver these somewhat tough years by being available and attentive. Though this is true at all the childhood stages, when our child enters the potentially awkward tween years, they deserve our full attention—not only to spot strengths but also to notice when something is amiss.

For our daughter Michaela, we almost missed the signs. As a tween, she enjoyed playing soccer at a competitive level. She loved her coach, and though he was hard on the team and pushed them to be their best, she respected him very much. The year he transitioned out was difficult for Michaela. The replacement coach was much younger and had a difficult time managing a team of preteen girls. Our daughter is a bit headstrong and direct, and this coach took offense at the bold questions she would ask during practice. Also, without our knowledge, the coach spoke against Michaela in some immature ways. This devastated our daughter. The light from her eyes dimmed, and we noticed her game performance steadily waned. When we asked her what happened to that spark, she wasn't willing to divulge her true hurt. We assumed she was growing out of the sport, but instead, we were missing vital parts of the story.

When we learned of the depth of the offense she had suffered, it took some serious intervention to help her through the damage to her self-image. Our daughter had not lost her Five E's for this sport; they had been sabotaged by a bad role model. Parents must practice being quick to listen and slow to speak. In this case, we missed the reason for the shift in our daughter's engagement.

Pay attention, dear parent. Many times, the story we've told ourselves about our children's behavior is not the true story. To engage our kids in their school years, we must stay in discovery mode. This helps prevent us from missing elements of the whole story and allows us to guide a child in their strengths even when others fail them.

Research and Development for Our Tweens

Parents are fascinated with newborns and toddlers, but now we enter a considerably definitive time to help our school-age child develop their strengths. Remember the drama of the reward-and-discipline model? Well, you'll be so glad to have made the shift to a research-and-development model by the time your kids are school age. Even if you are just starting to make this transition and your child is already 12, you will reap the benefits. We know from experience that it's never too late and is always worth the effort of changing from a frustrating model of parenting to one that nurtures the people God created our kids to become.

Our change toward strengths-based parenting required us to improve our communication. We had to exercise those essential skills of listening (and *really* hearing), asking questions, and waiting for answers. If we do all the talking or skim past what a child is saying or demonstrating with their behavior, we run the great risk of projecting our goals, strengths, and needs onto a developing child.

Jennifer Fox writes this in *Your Child's Strengths*:

> As we talk with our children about what they love and feel strong about, we need to be careful not to discuss our own aspirations or desires to mold and form them. Remain open. No one can tell you what your strengths are, and you cannot tell your children what their strengths are. They must tell you as a result of their own thinking process.[3]

Every day when Daniel and David come home from school, we get to ask them what made them feel strong. They know the question is coming, so they often arrive home ready to share. For example, one afternoon we might discover that David is excited about the science project he is working on and that Daniel feels strong because he gets to rehearse and perform the role of the wolf in the upcoming class play. As we've reinforced throughout this journey, staying engaged in discovery mode will reveal so much about the strengths your child is ready to develop.

The Three E's of Strength Development

Beyond asking the helpful question, "What makes you feel strong?" you can help your tween identify and develop their strengths by practicing the Three E's of strength development: engage, experiment, and encourage. These practices will serve you and your son or daughter throughout their teen years too. The Five E's help us notice a child's talent and natural ability and preferences. The Three E's are actions that allow us to help our kids deepen and expand their understanding of their strengths so they can grow in them.

Our change toward strengths-based parenting required us to improve our communication. We had to exercise those essential skills of listening (and *really* hearing), asking questions, and waiting for answers.

Engage

Ask questions about their interactions with others. Get involved in their connections with their teachers, coaches, aunts and uncles, grandparents, and any other influencers in their life. Find out what others see in different settings. Here are some questions you can ask your tween:

- How well do you relate to your teachers?
- What kind of questions do you ask the teacher?
- What does your teacher expect of you?
- How do you get the most from that relationship?

If your child is occasionally in the care of a babysitter or, as in our case, the child has been watched by their grandmother, here are additional questions:

- How do you get along with your care provider?
- What does she or he expect of you?
- What strengths do you experience when you are with the different caregivers in your life?

Next, ask questions of others who interact with your child. When your child spends the night at a friend's house, ask those parents what they see in your kid. Your children will often show different sides of themselves when they are around friends' parents or visiting relatives' homes—and certainly when they are in the classroom or on the sports field. The characteristics that emerge in these places provide clues and glimpses into who they are and will remind you just how much you have to learn about your kids.

Another reason we engage with our children's influential relationships is to better understand how we can partner with other adults. We have met with our kids' teachers to explain our strengths-based parenting approach and to understand how the teacher sees our children's strengths and non-strengths. We have found it's important to be an advocate for what we expect of our kids and to be the guardians of our kids' talents. We want each child to find places where they shine, and we enjoy those opportunities to share our delight with a child when we've witnessed another arena, setting, or relationship where they do just that.

Experiment

Try new things as a family. Take children to new places and expose them to new ways of seeing, learning, and interacting. A son or daughter's strengths might be quite different from our own, so if we stick to our tried-and-true favorites or hang out only with the same people, we are not introducing our child to tastes, sounds, sights, and personalities that might help them discover their strengths. New outings and activities and connections will pique curiosity and discovery.

We gleaned a lot of great information from an educational experiment. Our son David was assigned to do a science project in fourth grade. We explored possibilities together and discussed how cool it would be to find one that emphasized strengths. Then we read about the power of chess to improve reading and cognitive skills. Bingo. David called it the "Chess Affect" and posed this question: Could playing chess improve the reading or other scholastic abilities of school-age kids? David invited his eight-year-old brother, Daniel, to participate. (What older brother doesn't want to do experiments on his younger brother?) Daniel struggled with reading more than David did, so the project could potentially help both boys.

In brief, both boys played a chess match every day and watched a YouTube video about learning to play. Weekly, they took reading comprehension tests. We repeated this for several weeks until the project was due. The results? Of course, both boys improved their chess games considerably, but both boys also improved their reading ability! It was remarkable. What is exciting about an experiment is that it might yield benefits you didn't see coming. Even though Daniel didn't have as much interest in chess, he did like experiencing improvement and the opportunity to challenge and beat numerous contenders. This became a way to pique his natural ability *and* improve his learning capabilities.

Introducing a child to new experiences is a powerful way to identify and develop their emerging talents. This active step might lead you to museums or places where your child can do projects or attend extracurricular classes. Visit artisanal businesses or events where they can do clay work, sew, or experience different kinds of music. No matter what you do, keep those questions going. In fact, experimenting might lead to some of the best conversations you and your child have ever had. Here are some starters:

- Does this make you feel strong?
- Is this something that is bringing you energy?
- Is this something you look forward to going back and doing again?

Introducing a child to new experiences is a powerful way to identify and develop their emerging talents.

Encourage

Speak words that edify and build up your child. Keep them thinking of themselves through the framework of their talents. Inspire them to find ways to become experts in their own strengths. Think of ways to reinforce those behaviors that make them feel strong. You can verbally encourage your child or write notes or letters to place in their lunchbox. Take time to give them a hug, a high five, or a fist bump. Always find a way to connect with them when you see them excel.

Encouragement can include partnering with your child by setting the bar high. This isn't for every kid, but for the right personality, a challenge can be inspirational. It can feel like a vote of confidence from the family.

We set a high bar for David in his academics and encourage him to exceed his own expectations in his studies. Each time we set a high bar, such as attaining all As on his report card, David is motivated to work hard to reach this goal. We found that David was particularly encouraged when we took time to check in on his academic progress and comment on the success we observed.

As you see opportunities to build up your kids' abilities and strengths, be aware of the natural inclination to criticize or point out deficits. Focus instead on where your school-age child excels so you can edify them and encourage them to trust you. When you are speaking into their life, you want to give them the best of your energy and always provide a safe place in your presence. There, they can trust you and discover who they are and who they can become as a unique and loved child of God.

Confidence for the Next Stages

The years between cuddling a toddler and high-fiving a tween will go by quickly...and they matter greatly. This is when our kids are learning to form their friendships and trust their influencers, and we can help set the stage by reinforcing their confidence, helping them discover who they are, pointing out their competence and creativity, encouraging them to trust their knowledge, and opening doors so they can explore new horizons.

This is the time when our child is most impressionable and looking to us as leaders in their lives. This is the time to impress upon them that our relationship with them is a safe and caring place, that we are someone they can trust, and that we are in their corner and have their best interests at heart. This is the time to notice and nurture the shine in their eyes, the bounce in their step, and the smile on their face.

REVIEW THE PLAY

1. What have you learned about yourself as a parent from this chapter's exploration?

2. What is one way this chapter helped you make a shift toward playing to your child's God-given strengths?

3. What did you discover about your child this week that surprises you or changes the way you interact with them?

4. Which insight or activity from this chapter's Playbook offering is the most helpful to your family right now? Why?

Check out the activities for chapter 12 in the Parenting Playbook on page 203.

Train Teens and Empower Young Adults

The goal of parenting is to work yourself out of a job...to send young adults out into the world who are prepared to live as God's children.

PAUL DAVID TRIPP

The teen years usher in a new and complex stage in a child's development and our relationship with them. They will continue discovering personal preferences and abilities as well as who they are apart from their parents. Sons and daughters are stretching the limits of newfound strengths while often stretching boundaries—and their parents' patience. To maneuver this life season, many parents will lean toward one of two approaches to handling and shaping their teen: command and control or motivation and inspiration.

Command and Control

I (Brandon) grew up in a home where I was expected to do as I was told when I was told. If the directive was "Jump," we were expected to answer, "How high?" This slightly military approach was based on a system of commands and resulted in either compliance or consequences. My parents were very loving and supportive; this method of leadership was simply an extension of their experience.

So it isn't surprising that when I was a young father with teens, this was my go-to method of leading my family. I often told my teen son or daughter what to do. If they didn't comply, I'd tell them again with more force. If this went on another round, I would express the directive with stronger force and explain the consequences for noncompliance. This eliminated most back talk, but it also eliminated collaboration or negotiation.

You've probably been there. Let's be honest, parent to parent—the command-and-control method has its place. Our teens need to listen to us as we give them instructions to protect and guide them. I had my teens' best interests at heart, but I now recognize how often I was responding from fear. I was afraid they might make poor choices and I might lose control. As their responsibilities and risks grew, so did my concerns.

The Cost of Command and Control

Even on the best days, when our teens were complying, we could see the wind of interest leave their sails the minute they acquiesced instead of expressing themselves. Raising my voice to get compliance did not encourage Bailee to listen to me. She told me what I wanted to hear but often said it with a tone that betrayed her frustration, hurt, or anger. She began responding with rote or even passive-aggressive behavior. And when her eyes met mine, the light of engagement had disappeared. I didn't know about a strengths-based approach to life or parenting back then, but I did know I was losing my connection to Bailee. Analyn and I wanted more for our relationship with our teens.

We don't recall the specific moment that a command-and-control (or out-of-control) moment revealed its shortcomings, but thankfully we eventually started paying attention to the cost of this parenting style. We had set up a system of consequences all right—but we were *all* paying them. Relationships forged in this dynamic become transactional rather than relational, and as a result, countless parents reside with teens they never really get to know.

I've heard one parent say that it's not a question of *if* your teen will lie to you; it's *how often* they will lie to you. If there's truth to this, wouldn't it be better to form a relationship of trust with our teens so they feel safe coming to us when they fail, when they aren't strong? I lost some important years of getting to know my older kids in the way I was able to connect with our younger set. Since then, I have invested time getting to know who each of our older kids is, and I'm sharing who I am as well. Healing can come, but first we must realize something has been lost.

Growing as a Parent

We are thankful that as we engaged in a strengths-based approach, we realized that changes were needed. This opened the door to more health with our oldest, Bailee. Our growth as parents was evident in our relationship with our second-born, Lance. We knew that as he entered his teens, he would push against authority and want to exert his control over his own outcomes. We prepared to meet his journey with a more relational approach. Growth and change are not easy. Transformation didn't occur overnight, but in time we became more emotionally and spiritually available to our teens.

Our new convictions were challenged the day Lance declared he was going to initiate a dating relationship that he knew we were not in favor of. After listening to the reasons he wanted to date the girl, our first response was, "Absolutely not." This led to a heightened interaction with our son, but thankfully, cooler heads prevailed. We decided to leave the interaction for some time to think and pray through our response.

This was our son's first real, direct challenge to our authority. We could tell there was more on the line than just dating this young lady, and we needed to measure our response in light of the bigger picture. Our gut reaction was to immediately forbid him to pursue the relationship and then limit his driving privileges as an extra measure of assurance. We even considered removing his mobile phone privileges just to show him who really was in control.

We allowed some time to pass and took a few breaths while the initial anger and frustration subsided. Through prayer, it became clear that teens need to learn some things by going through the process on their own. Just like us, a teen will learn through their successes as well as their failures. This perspective calmed us, and we reentered the conversation without judgment or the need to command and control our son.

As we spoke to Lance, we expressed our concerns, encouraged him to pay attention to the potential pitfalls in front of him, and then gave him permission to move forward with his decision.

The relationship indeed proved to be a poor fit. Watching our concerns play out was difficult; however, the experience shaped the way Lance would think about future relationships. And our open communication established a foundation that felt safe and honest.

We grow as parents and help our teens grow as people by learning to communicate during the tough stuff. Amid conflict and loss or in a standoff of strong emotions or differing opinions, we do well to remember to remain calm and clearheaded. There is the hope of a clear path through a difficult topic.

Reframing Rebellion

As a parent of teens coming out of their adolescent years, remember that this is when our kids are going to have moments of rebellion. Jennifer Fox says the stereotypical story of rebellion doesn't need to be true. There is hope for our teens to be healthier if we view them and what they are going through with empathy and through the lens of strengths.

> I am able to look at most acts of rebellion and see a positive and healthy desire that was turned on its ear. When adults look closely, they will see how fresh and original—how open to discovering life's meaning—young people really are…Up until the onslaught of [adolescent] hormones, children grow with various societal and cultural influences but without an organized sense of self. In their adolescent years, kids become aware of themselves as separate and powerful people who have choices in their development. This can be exhilarating at times and overwhelming at others. Hormones awaken and release for the first time the deeply encoded messages about life and death, purpose and meaning, love and rage. Adolescents live in a state of

heightened awareness, searching for something bigger than they are to mirror their yearnings for significance...They long to know that the world wants them and that life has, in fact, been waiting for their arrival. This is not a rebellion, this is a strengths awakening.[1]

Motivation and Inspiration for Your Teen

Reframing rebellion helps adults and teens respond to circumstances with hope. Our shift to using motivation and inspiration more often than command and control kept us watching for each child's strengths and for ways to nurture those strengths. This collaborative approach invited us to listen, learn, and move our teen toward the outcome that is designed for them instead of the one that feels right to us. That was and is a huge shift. Our endgame is not what is best for us; it's what is best for each teen's personal path with God.

Motivation requires learning what compels kids at this stage in their lives, even if they are still figuring this out. According to Dr. Waters, "At this time, teenagers get a more precise sense of their strengths. Your role is to help your child put more effort and time into systematically developing his strengths."[2]

Our endgame is not what is best for us; it's what is best for each teen's personal path with God.

Partnering as a Parent

When Lance and Ciera were in high school, we partnered with them to launch a youth group through our local church. Every Wednesday evening, we opened our home to the group, and Ciera and Lance helped us serve. We hoped to use this opportunity to provide a strength-building experience for our teens and serve others as a family. What unfolded surpassed even those hopes.

Lance was developing his guitar-playing skills and his vocal strength, and he learned to lead a small group in worship. He was also able to casually mentor other teens interested in music and leadership. He took it upon himself to hold rehearsals on an additional evening of the week and invested significant time into the youth who joined the band with him.

Ciera served by sharing her testimony and encouragement with the youth group and participating on the leadership team. She was influential with her peer group and invited several of her friends to join her on Wednesday evenings. Some of those friends continued in their faith and service and even went on to serve in the youth group after high school graduation.

We look back on those years and marvel at the grace of God leading us to rethink our parenting approach and transition from primarily command and control to motivation and inspiration. This shift had an amazing impact, helping all our children think about their strengths in relation to the Great Commission:

> All authority in heaven and on earth has been given to me. Therefore go and make disciples of all nations, baptizing them in the name of the Father and of the Son and of the Holy Spirit, and teaching them to obey everything I have commanded you. And surely I am with you always, to the very end of the age (Matthew 28:18-20).

Our younger kids watched as their older siblings developed their strengths and confidence through service and made a difference among their peers. It made such an impression on Madeline and Michaela that now, as young teens, they requested we restart the youth group. Now on Wednesday nights, our family is hosting and serving another wave of teens.

Michaela's eyes shine as she uses her strengths to plan and lead the youth group in fun interactive games and engage with her peers in small-group discussions. Madeline uses her strengths to show hospitality to our guests as she prepares food and baked goods for everyone. For a youth event held on Saint Patrick's Day, Madeline took it upon herself to make green cupcakes with candy rainbows and little candy pots of gold. They were a hit. As proud partners with our teens, we've watched them embark on the adventure of developing their strengths to serve others in love. This is the ultimate expression of strengths-based parenting we hope for.

Keep your eyes and heart open for ways to partner with your teens and help them serve others. Get creative. Maybe your family chooses a community outreach program or local nonprofit to support with time and finances. Perhaps you could host a regular game night for your kids' friends and others so the teens have something to do that is interactive and fun in a home that is safe and welcoming. There are so many options—let your child's strengths lead the way. In the Parenting Playbook, we provide you with further ideas to consider in partnering with your teens.

Developing Strength of Character

We lead our teens to greater maturity when we motivate and inspire them to use their strengths and build their character. Here are three ways they can develop both:

- serving others with their strengths
- submitting to authority
- stepping up and taking responsibility

Serving Others with Their Strengths

Expand your teen's vision for the future by reminding them that talents are entrusted to them to invest in the lives of others. It is a mark of maturity when our kids leverage their strengths for the benefit of others. Give your child this verse as a mission statement to begin: "In everything I did, I showed you that by this kind of hard work we must help the weak, remembering the words the Lord Jesus himself said: 'It is more blessed to give than to receive'" (Acts 20:35).

On a recent trip, we were teaching this principle to a group of teens while serving a large gathering: meal preparation, serving food, cleanup, room setup for teaching times, and so on. All the teens were developing strengths (or maybe noticing them for the first time) as they conducted the chores. We discussed how this is what leadership looks like.

Teens develop their talents when they serve others in love—in a class, working after school, or participating in sports, music, or youth events. When your teen starts to serve in their strengths and with integrity, they won't be the only one who changes for the better.

We recently watched a video with our teens about a young man who started a movement in his high school by looking for kids who were eating alone in the lunchroom and sitting beside them. He was inspired by his early years as a young immigrant from Port-au-Prince, Haiti, who knew no one and who often sat alone and felt alone. The We Dine Together movement exists to encourage others to get to know new students and connect with those who are often on the perimeter.[3]

When your teen starts to serve in their strengths and with integrity, they won't be the only one who changes for the better.

Submitting to Authority

We started this list focusing on service because once a child begins using their abilities to serve, the concept of submission is easier to comprehend and embrace. Submission is a rare quality, making it more important to model for our kids. As they grow beyond the childhood years, they are ready to engage their strengths in a more constructive way. They have more control over their emotions and can grasp different ways to use their strengths to benefit others and learn from leaders. It's the opportune time to teach our teens to become good employees, team members, family members, citizens, and students and to lean on foundational attributes of respect, humility, integrity, and conviction of faith.

It won't take much life experience before your child realizes that not all leaders are strong ones. However, they can learn how to show respect for each leader or teacher and take away important lessons. Sometimes the lessons are what *not* to do; sometimes the lessons are about how to engage and listen when you have an opinion a boss or coach doesn't agree with. Help your teen learn to express their opinion in a respectful way. You'll know on the home front whether they are catching on to this skill. Model for your child how to ask good questions to engage in dialogue that leads toward a positive outcome. Point out how strength is evident through submission. It's a tough skill for most of us, so encourage your teen each time you see them living out a heart of submission.

"After discovering more about my strengths, I was able to understand why I operate the way I do and to approach certain tasks or problems more effectively. I grew as a better person and employee."

—LANCE (24)

Stepping Up and Taking Responsibility

A young child *might* get away with passing blame for a misstep on a sibling or another kid in their class, but the teenage years are when kids learn to take responsibility for mistakes as well as successes. When Lance was a teenager, we purchased a truck and agreed to sell it to him for half of what we paid for it. Lance decided to trade the truck he had purchased from us and buy another vehicle—without telling us. (Welcome to the teen brain.)

On the appointed day, he met with the seller and signed in *my* (Brandon's) name. When he arrived home with his "new" vehicle and proudly announced that he had bartered the deal, I asked how this was accomplished without my signature. He confessed to the forgery. I paused to take a breath and think about the consequences he would face. Instead of allowing my emotions to get the better of me, I explained that he needed to step up and take responsibility for his decisions.

Unfortunately, the exchange did not work in his favor, and he was the unhappy owner of an undrivable car. He felt betrayed by the other person. His focus could have remained there, but we reminded him that he was ultimately responsible for the action and the consequences. I was proud of how my son set out to remedy the situation by saving his money, investing in a drivable vehicle, and purchasing his own insurance.

Encourage your teen and discuss what it looks like to step up and take responsibility. Nearly every life experience will be a training ground for this lesson, including when they make any significant decision—where to live, where to work, how to manage their money, and which relationships to build. As a result, your teen will become a young adult who is ready to brave their new world of challenges and choices with bright, shining eyes, able to see their next steps with clarity and conviction.

Partnering with our teens and engaging them in adult conversations was and is our greatest learning opportunity and greatest challenge as parents. At this age and stage, our approach to development shifted. Rather than giving specific guidance, we now practice side-by-side leadership and development. As our teens grew into young adults, we entered the season of learning to parent with permission.

Empowering Young Adults

We've witnessed the fruit of the strengths-based approach in the lives of our young adults. Each is confident of who they are, what they can accomplish, and how they might use their strengths to impact their world in their work, family life, and service to God. They are amazingly raw, real, open, approachable, humble, and honest—making them confidently vulnerable about who they are and who they're not. Such self-awareness allows a maturing person to view themselves and others without judgment.

Our young adults are currently Bailee, Lance, Ciera, and their respective spouses—Jordan, Christine, and Adam. We pray that each child will not simply roll along with the world but will change it by living a courageous life empowered by the strengths God gave them.

From our perspective, empowering our young adults started all the way back when they were small children. We were responsible for giving them clear messages as to what we expected from them and how they would develop their strengths and faith to lead successful, fulfilled lives in service of others. To cement this message along the way, we endeavored to model the behavior we hoped to inspire in our kids. We took this to be our greatest challenge as parents, because as every leader knows, the true test of leadership comes from the mirror. We speak the message, model the way, and expect the model to be mirrored back to us.

We pray that each child will not simply roll along with the world but will change it by living a courageous life empowered by the strengths God gave them.

The mirror test is constantly challenged through the tween and teen years as our kids' behavior sometimes contrasts with our message and model. Yet with introspection, often the behavior we see in the mirror is the behavior we inadvertently modeled. The adage "Do what I say and not what I do" simply does not work.

If we want to raise adults whose eyes shine with a strong faith, a clear grasp of their strengths, and an understanding of how to apply those strengths in their calling and career, we must model the way for them to follow. Every loving parent wants to do the best possible job to wisely launch their young adult into the world to make an impact. For a successful transition to take place, our parenting role also needs to adapt. Here are five launch codes of conduct that will help you do just that.

The Launch Codes of Conduct

Relate as Adults

We've discovered the gift of an adult relationship with our grown kids based on trust, nurtured each time we listen to them, learn from them, and laugh with them. We look for ways to engage with them in their careers, callings, and challenges. We learn to be their friends and their parents at the same time. And always, we give them the space they deserve to grow into who they are becoming and to make their own decisions.

One day, one of our in-law children came to me (Brandon) with an important matter and divulged some personal information about a struggle. With permission, I shared it with Analyn, and she reminded me it was a great privilege for us to be entrusted with personal needs from our in-law children. She highlighted the way our in-law children trust us and the acceptance they feel as members of our family. As I considered the situation and prayed for words of wisdom, I felt the gravity and gratitude of relating to my children and their spouses as adults.

If your child marries, welcome the spouse into the family with respect and trust. When they are made to feel like an add-on instead of a member of the family, they will always function as an add-on. Integrate them into the family. As Christians, we believe that in Christ, a husband and wife become one flesh (Ephesians 5:31-32). Therefore, the spouse who is added to your family is as much your son or daughter as your own flesh and blood.

Respect Their Autonomy

To be an effective parent for your young adult, two items are essential: preserving their autonomy and showing them respect. Believe me, this serves you and them. Set the parameters of the relationship while establishing your boundaries as well. Be careful not to manipulate them. Invite them to meals, holidays, and vacations, but do this with an open hand. Think of each invitation as an offering, a true gift rather than an obligation that binds your adult child to your wishes.

Lance has been a diehard fan of the Philadelphia Eagles his whole life. The Eagles made it to the Super Bowl in 2018, so I (Brandon) was looking forward to watching the game with him. I also kept in mind that Lance might want to watch it with his friends instead. I let him know that his mom and I and some family friends would be having a Super Bowl party and that he was invited. I added that we knew he'd have options, so it was an open invite. Lance later called to say he'd join us. I could tell he appreciated how the invitation was presented.

Most parents want so badly to spend time with their kids, especially when grandchildren come along. We need to prevent that well-intentioned longing from nudging us toward any form of manipulation to make them feel bad if they don't come over or make space in their week for us to visit. Establishing rapport with our adult children through trust and truth is more important than getting our way at their expense.

Reserve Your Opinion Until Asked

Healthy communication is key for all these launch codes of conduct. When we respect our grown child's process of making decisions, we preserve trust. This will make it easier for them to come to us with their ideas or concerns. Sometimes they just want a sounding board; other times they want advice. Always clarify, "Would you like my advice on the matter? Would you like me to offer you my perspective?" And if they say no, be fine with that. Don't forget that they're sharing as an adult.

Establishing rapport with our adult children
through trust and truth is more important
than getting our way at their expense.

Well-meaning parents want to warn their adult kids of potential pitfalls. You can warn them without needing to save them. Young adults must make their own mistakes, and parents must make their own mistakes as well. We have learned the subtle art of waiting to be asked for our perspective or asking whether our opinion is wanted at the time.

Some time ago, two of our adult kids went through a challenging situation in their local church. As the situation unfolded, we waited for them to come to us if they had questions. We too had endured some difficult circumstances at a local church, so we had insight to share, but our priority was to listen, learn, and respect their position.

When our daughter did ask for our opinion, we gladly discussed our perspective and experience while showing respect for her decision-making process. She appreciated our advice and was able to take a step back and make an informed decision with her husband.

Remember to Pray for Them

Praying is an awesome responsibility. And believe us, even your grown child will find comfort knowing you're partnering with them through prayer for their every need and for their strengths to be used for their calling. As our children grow and mature, we can be their greatest intercessors. "The prayer of a righteous person is powerful and effective" (James 5:16), and that power is ours when we remember our kids before the throne of our Father in heaven.

We believe God gives insight to pray about an area before things happen. And daily, we can pray over foundational aspects of our children's lives, including God's protection, providence, favor, grace, and guidance. We've experienced the gift of being directed to certain Scriptures to share with our kids for encouragement and as reminders that his words are always relevant to their lives.

Your grown child will find comfort knowing you're partnering with them through prayer for their every need and for their strengths to be used for their calling.

As Ciera graduated from college and prepared for her first career job, she and Adam considered the direction they would take. During this season, she sought us out for our wisdom and perspective. We carefully weighed the choices with her and then committed to pray for her as she thought through her decision. One Saturday, as I (Brandon) enjoyed a quiet morning in our house, I was prompted to pray for Ciera and send her a text with some encouragement and a Scripture verse to comfort her as she contemplated her next move. When she read her text, she was grateful for the message, the prayers, and the Scripture. We believe the prayers of a parent can be one of a young adult's strongest sources of encouragement.

Remain Fascinated

The fascination for your child that you've cultivated throughout the years won't and shouldn't end when you launch them into the world as an independent young adult. Your relationship will change with the new boundaries and expectations, but there is also a new freedom to experience your child as a friend and maybe as a leader. Do you know the saying "The student is now the teacher"? You might be surprised to see how the strengths you once watched for, played to, and championed in your child are now fully developed and inspire and inform their life.

A while back, Lance began to consider some new financial options for his family. After he had done significant research, he shared some of his findings with us. In the following weeks, we asked more questions, and he provided more information. Throughout our exchanges, we told Lance his acquisition of knowledge was helping us reconsider our own perspectives and take some new steps. As we complimented the way he put his strengths into action and conveyed how proud we were of him, we saw his shining eyes. And he saw ours.

The gift of remaining fascinated with your adult child is that you'll be encouraged by the ideas they share and the directions they choose. This fascination helps you be patient and ask questions before trying to address what you think they need. Your curiosity enhances your role as an advocate who develops and encourages their strengths by pointing out areas of maturity.

We promise that when you see your grown child's unique heart and abilities in action, your fascination will grow into admiration for the person God created and you've been blessed to parent. Be encouraged… play to their strengths and pray for their strengths to shine brightly in the adult they are becoming. This is the privilege, calling, and joy of the parenting life.

———————— **REVIEW THE PLAY** ————————

1. What have you learned about yourself as a parent from this chapter's exploration?

2. What is one way this chapter helped you make a shift toward playing to your child's God-given strengths?

3. What did you discover about your child this week that surprises you or changes the way you interact with them?

4. Which insight or activity from this chapter's Playbook offering is the most helpful to your family right now? Why?

Check out the activities for chapter 13 in the Parenting Playbook on page 207.

The Parenting Playbook

A playbook helps us put plans and ideas into action. That's why we are excited to provide you with this playbook of activities, questions, and inspirations for your *Play to Their Strengths* learning journey. We want the insights of each chapter to become real in your home and in your lives.

Here are some hints to help you make your way through the Playbook:

1. Give yourself time to read each Playbook offering so you can plan ahead for any family activities it suggests.

2. Take time to pray before you look at each chapter's offering.

3. If you can, plan a weekend away to read through the chapters. Then map out the days or weeks when you will engage your child with the activities and questions from the book and the Playbook.

4. If you go through this book as a couple, share with each other your answers to the "Review the Play" questions at the close of the chapter and your answers and comments for each Playbook section.

5. Numerous lists, charts, and other resources featured in the

Playbook are available at www.analynbrandon.com. We will continue adding resources to our site, so visit often.

6. We encourage you to record your answers and observations. Use your own journal or see our website for information about ordering the *Play Journal* we have created to complement *Play to Their Strengths.*

Also, here are some tips for using the Parenting Playbook with a small group:

1. Create an agreement of support and trust for the group.

2. Set a plan that allows everyone to take time with each chapter and the corresponding Playbook offering. For example, a small group might decide to meet on the first week to get to know each other and discuss the first chapter, followed by six weeks in which your group discusses two chapters and Playbook sections per week.

3. Complete the exercises in advance so the group time can be focused on sharing insights from that experience.

4. Be sensitive when sharing about your children so that you respect their privacy as individuals. Talk in advance with your child to determine those safe boundaries.

5. Consider starting the time together by having everyone share a response to one of the "Review the Play" questions from the chapter.

6. More resources for group leaders, including a companion video series, are available at www.analynbrandon.com under the resource section.

INSPIRE YOUR KIDS TO SHINE

Adjusting our vision to see the shine in our kids' eyes took some time. We had to peer through the haze of their actions and attitudes. Yet as we trained ourselves to watch for that look of delight and engagement, we noticed it in each of our kids at different times. For Bailee it was on the stage. For Lance it was taking apart a toy and inventing something new.

Your turn. Think of a time when you saw the shine in your child's eyes—at any age. If you have a teen and can recall a time when their eyes were shining at age six, then note that. This is more than a one-time expression of delight; it's the look that returns each time your child is doing an activity, describing what they did, or planning to do it again. Below are some ways to notice shining eyes in kids of each age range. In your journal, respond to these prompts for each child.

Children of Any Age

1. I first saw my child's eyes light up when...

2. I'm not sure when my child's eyes have shined, but this has started me thinking that...

Toddlers

Playtime provides an excellent opportunity to notice shining eyes. Do you see it when they play with a certain toy, watch certain programs, or listen to particular stories? If your children are past this stage, take a moment to look back and reflect. What seemed to attract their attention?

School Age

Consider your child's engagement in certain school subjects and extracurricular activities. Watch your child interact with new forms of technology. Perhaps there is a video game your kiddo is especially fond of. Which genres of games or what forms of (authorized) social media fascinate them? Talk with your child about school, sports, art pursuits, entertainment choices, and so on. Be specific: "What is it about [activity] you like so much? What part of [subject] suits your interests right now?"

Teens

This is the time when interests could become really clear—or when the journey becomes a bit challenging. Teens have more choices and more autonomy to discover what makes their eyes shine. School, sports, clubs, bands, recreation, relationships, jobs, and hobbies can present opportunities to witness them in their element. If your teen isn't openly sharing about their interests, call out their strengths to encourage them while also giving them time and space.

Young Adults

We think of this stage as starting in the senior year of high school. From a responsibility standpoint, your child might start earlier or later. The hope is that at this stage, you *and* your young adult have a good idea of what makes their eyes shine. Perhaps it was revealed in the major they selected for college. Or perhaps in a cause they serve and support.

Questions for Kids

Ask your kids to answer the first two questions and complete the sentence for number 3. Write down their answers for further consideration.

1. What is your favorite activity to do during the day?
2. What sorts of things do you feel most successful at?
3. How would you complete this sentence? I feel most confident when...

Questions for You

1. Did you confirm something you already knew about your child? If so, what?

2. In what way have you been living out a myth rather than a mission?

3. Why are you ready now to embrace the mission for your parenting and your family?

EXCHANGE FRUSTRATION FOR FASCINATION

What are you afraid of? In chapter 2, we share that we were initially fascinated with our littles ones, but then we began being motivated by fear. We didn't want to get it wrong, so we compensated by trying to do everything we could to look like we had it all together. Truth be told, this was no picnic. We envisioned people thinking about us in negative ways. We imagined what they would say about us when we left a party or the event. Are you as afraid of failing as a parent as we were?

Take a few moments and jot down some of your fears. Start with some of the clear fears we all have—that our children will suffer illness, injury, or other pain. That they won't fit in. That they will be "that kid" who seems to constantly misbehave. Are you afraid of missing the mark by involving them in the wrong activities or enrolling them in the wrong school? What comes to mind? Write down your thoughts in your journal.

Now confront fear with faith. Read these Bible passages and consider how each one gives you a truth about fear or faith.

This is the truth I will trust:

> There is no fear in love. But perfect love drives out fear, because fear has to do with punishment. The one who fears is not made perfect in love. We love because he first loved us (1 John 4:18-19).

This is the truth I will trust:

> Rejoice in the Lord always. I will say it again: Rejoice!...

> Do not be anxious about anything, but in every situation, by prayer and petition, with thanksgiving, present your requests to God. And the peace of God, which transcends all understanding, will guard your hearts and your minds in Christ Jesus (Philippians 4:4,6-7).

This is the truth I will trust:

> I lift up my eyes to the mountains—where does my help come from? My help comes from the LORD, the Maker of heaven and earth. He will not let your foot slip—he who watches over you will not slumber; indeed, he who watches over Israel will neither slumber nor sleep. The LORD watches over you—the LORD is your shade at your right hand; the sun will not harm you by day, nor the moon by night. The LORD will keep you from all harm—he will watch over your life; the LORD will watch over your coming and going both now and forevermore (Psalm 121).

Red Flag of Frustration

For each child, write down the red flags of frustration that arise because of what they *do*. Then immediately after writing down the red flags, write down their *who*. How do you see your child's identity shine through? Here's an example:

Child's name: Ciera
Red flag: challenging with questions and debated decision
Who she is: a leader who has qualities to influence others
    for good

Child's name:
Red flag:
Who she is:

Child's name:
Red flag:
Who he is:

LIVE IN DISCOVERY MODE

Each year, my (Analyn's) real estate team spends a day making vision boards. We do this to remind ourselves what's most important in our lives and to visualize what we're aiming toward in the coming year. This activity centers me and grows my appreciation of each team member.

We started to do this activity as a family to help each child better understand themselves and to give us insight into their lives. It also makes for a great weekend activity. Below is a list of supplies to prepare before you begin.

Vision Board Supplies

- Poster board—one for each member of the family.

- Magazines and periodicals you don't mind being cut up—include a wide assortment: fashion, home, sports, travel, history, nature, city based, tech, and so on.

- Scissors—one pair for each child is best. Supervise little ones.

- Tape or glue sticks—tape is cleaner, but glue gets the job done as well.

- Colored pens, markers, colored pencils, and crayons.

- Stickers, borders, printed images...ask your kids what other art supplies they might want, such as fabric, ribbon, metallic pens, or glitter!

Create Your Vision Board

Let your family know which day and time to anticipate the activity. Here are the basics to share and ask when you are about to begin. To make this activity enjoyable and rewarding, don't give too much instruction or coaching. Let them play.

- A vision board can be about the future, such as what you want to be when you grow up, but it can also be about the past and the present.

- What fun memories do you have?

- What do you enjoy doing the most?

- How do you see yourself, and how do others see you?

- The only rule is to make the board a positive expression of you.

- There is no wrong way to do the boards. We'll be sharing these with each other and hanging these in our home where we can be reminded of what we learned about each other today.

Play some fun background music and get started! Participate with your children and engage with them during the presentation time.

Instructions When Presenting the Vision Boards

- Parents go first. Set the tone by sharing your personal insights. Let the kids ask why you selected certain pictures or words or phrases that represent you.

- Ask the kids to share their boards. As they share, let them go all the way through their board before asking questions.

- Stay positive. This is an excellent chance to learn about who your child is and what they think about their past, present, and future.

- After each child has presented, let other family members ask clarifying questions. Make sure to monitor the questions and comments to guide the commentary in a positive direction.

- Note in your journal what you hear from each of your kids. As you ask questions, stay in discovery mode. Look for nuggets of information about each child you can use later. For example, if your daughter shares photos of nature and tells you she loves to be outdoors, schedule time to go for a hike along a nature trail.

Actionable intel is powerful. Schedule time to follow up with each of your kids to learn more about them. If it doesn't make it onto our calendars, it doesn't get done. Using this family activity to plan events is key to success. Explore new museums, purchase books on particular subjects of interest, watch documentaries of time periods that apply, enroll them in a new class or activity you found out they had an interest in, volunteer for a cause your children highlight in the vision boards, start a nonprofit, research a new country or city of interest...the list is endless. Most important, consider how you can encourage each child to discover who God has created them to be. How you can support that discovery?

IDENTIFY AND
HONOR THEIR STRENGTHS

The Five E's are so helpful for identifying natural talents and the greatest potential for strengths. Sit down with each of your kids and go through the activity with them. Interview them or have them fill in answers in your journal. Let them answer first. If they get stuck, feel free to share what you have noticed about them.

Identifying the Five E's

Enthusiasm

- What are you naturally drawn to?
- What do you enjoy, and why do you enjoy it?
- What is it about the activity that captures your attention?

Ease

- What comes easy to you?
- Is there a subject or activity you have picked up quickly?
- What do you seem to innately know the steps to and be able to engage in effortlessly?

Excellence

- Where do you see a standout ability that separates you from average engagement and aptitude?

- Who has validated your performance?
- What awards have you earned for outstanding performance?

Energy

- What energizes you?
- What activities leave you feeling depleted?
- For which activities do you seem to have an endless reserve of energy?

Enjoyment

- Which finished tasks, assignments, or projects give you the greatest long-term satisfaction?
- What do you enjoy so much that you will press through difficulties to do it?
- Which activities do you take the most pride in accomplishing?

Now that you've worked through these questions with your child, list three things he or she does that connect to all Five E'S.

Identifying Your Child's Strengths

I (Brandon) developed a list of strengths for you to consider as you investigate the Five E's and help you identify the strengths of your child. This inventory of strengths is based on years of observation with our children as well as insights I've gained over 15 years working with individuals and organizations as a strengths-based development expert. This list isn't meant to be exhaustive, but it will provide you with a jumping-off point toward discovery and development.

To access the strengths inventory for parents to assess their kids, visit www.analynbrandon.com and look for the free resource section. Once you have located this section, follow the instruction and enter the password PLAY to access the inventory of strengths for kids. If you have any questions or challenges with these instructions, please email brandon@analynbrandon.com, and we will provide you with assistance.

After you have completed working your way through the strengths inventory, we recommend setting aside time to discuss the strengths with your child. This is an opportunity for you to understand how your child views himself or herself in light of the strengths you identified in them.

UNCOVER THEIR CALLING

We truly believe that each of our kids has a unique calling from the Lord and that we are responsible for helping them discover this calling. Ask your child the following questions and write the answers in your journal. If your kids are also keeping a journal, have them record this too.

1. What kind of person do you want to be?
2. What do you want to be known for?
3. How do you want others to describe you?

Path to Greatness for Your Kid

Based on the answers to these questions, take some time to explore with your child their potential path to greatness. Have them think through each step of this path and write their responses.

1. List some successes you've had. Why have you experienced success in those areas?
2. Think about life right here, right now. In what ways are you successful now?
3. Look ahead. What might the future hold for you? How can you be successful in the future?

ACTIVATE THE RIPPLE EFFECT

We are always amazed at the impact one life can have on another. We love to watch our children learn to see outside of themselves and serve others. This teaches them humility, kindness, and most importantly, a deep love for others.

The pebble in the pond image we discuss in chapter 6 is a way to illustrate the idea that your kids' lives will have an impact on others. When you teach your kids about service as a positive way to utilize their strengths, they will grow in maturity and be more likely to use their talents to benefit others.

Pebble in the Pond Activity

For this activity, show your child the graphic below or re-create it on a separate piece of paper or a poster board. You could even leave off the labels, explain the ripple effect to your child, and ask him or her to suggest names for the ever-widening circles of influence. Next, have your child write a response to this question for each group: "How could I use my strengths to serve this group and have an impact?"

World

Community

School

Friends

Family

Me

SEEK *YOUR* SUPER

By now we have made some real progress in understanding this idea of focusing on strengths, staying in discovery mode, and learning more about our kids. We hope you're feeling stronger as a parent and ready to lean in to *your* strengths and make them stronger. For this next play in the Playbook, we ask you to answer the two questions posed in the chapter. Write your answers here or in your journal.

1. Do I allow my daily activities—work, school, chores, bills, and so on—to overshadow my exuberance and joy?

2. Do I allow the realities of life to overshadow my child's exuberance and joy?

We can all easily slip into this state of distraction. The world is a tough place, life has challenges, and we can find ourselves feeling in over our heads. This is why we need to know our strengths! It's time to investigate the inventory of parenting strengths found at www.analynbrandon.com in the free resource section. Once you have located the section, enter the password STRENGTHS and locate your strengths in the inventory provided.

Overcoming Imposter Syndrome

As we wrote in chapter 7, when parents suffer from imposter syndrome, their lack of confidence makes it more difficult for children to follow them. To protect you from this happening in your life, we encourage you to share your list of parenting strengths with your family. Show your list to your spouse and kids. Let them comment on what they see in you. Take their comments to heart. In business, this sort of activity is called a 360-degree survey, and it provides great feedback for leaders. Having this knowledge will allow you to adjust the list and consider steps for growing in your strengths.

As you consider your parenting strengths, keep in mind the areas that are clearly not strengths for you. We will give attention to these in chapter 9.

DON'T BUY THE LIES

To underscore the truths and lies discussed in chapter 8, explore this activity with your school-age kids so they can feel the difference between doing an activity from a place of strength and doing it from a place of weakness. As with each Playbook exercise, we encourage you to go through the activity first or at least at the same time as your child. We've written the instructions below so you can read them to your kids. Have each child complete the activity in their own journal or on a separate piece of paper.

Handwriting Challenge

> We are going to do a short challenge. Everyone needs a pen or pencil for this challenge. List numbers one through five on your paper. Now, when I say go, your challenge is to write your name five times in 30 seconds. As a part of this challenge, we're going to work on an area of non-strength. So...please hold up your pen or pencil...now switch hands. When I say go, write your name—first and last—with your nondominant hand. Ready...set...go!

Debrief: Once you call time, ask the following questions:

1. How did you feel doing that activity?

2. If you had to do your homework using your nondominant hand, how would you like that?

3. Do think you would get better at writing with your nondominant hand?

4. Do you think you would wish you could return to writing with your dominant hand? Why?

5. How would this situation make you feel?

The consensus is usually that writing with their nondominant hand is frustrating or annoying. When asked if they could improve, the answer is usually yes, and this is true; they would improve. However, when asked about why they would wish to use their dominant hand, most kids respond that using their dominant hand makes them feel better or stronger because it feels natural to them.

Round Two

This time, we're adding a little twist. When I say go, write your name five times in 30 seconds using the hand you usually use for writing. Ready...set...go!

Debrief: After this round of writing, ask your child these questions:

1. Describe the difference you felt between round one and round two.

2. Why do you think you felt that way?

3. If you had a choice to use your nondominant hand or your strong hand, which one would you prefer?

4. Do you think you could get more done with your strong hand?

5. Do you think you would be more confident? Why?

Discuss the difference between using strengths and non-strengths. Then have each child list eight things he or she is naturally good at (like "writing with my strong hand") and eight things he or she is not naturally good at (like "writing with my nondominant hand").

Getting Stronger

Let's review the formula from the chapter for growing a talent into a strength.

$$\begin{array}{rl} & \textbf{Talent} \quad \text{(a natural ability)} \\ \times & \underline{\textbf{Investment} \quad \text{(learning, practicing, developing)}} \\ = & \textbf{Strength} \quad \text{(something that comes easily and makes} \\ & \qquad\qquad\quad \text{you feel strong)} \end{array}$$

Now use this equation with one or two items on your child's "naturally good at" list. Include the investment factors for a practical way to grow a strength. For example...

$$\begin{array}{rl} & \textbf{Talent} \quad \text{I'm naturally good at singing.} \\ \times & \underline{\textbf{Investment} \quad \text{I will invest in this by joining the}} \\ & \qquad\qquad\quad \text{school choir and practicing at home.} \\ = & \textbf{Strength} \quad \text{When I am strong, I will be able to serve} \\ & \qquad\qquad\quad \text{on the church worship team.} \end{array}$$

To boost your child's motivation, encourage him or her to create a chart like this to track progress and watch talents grow into strengths:

	Investment	How I'm Stronger
Week 1		
Week 2		
Week 3		
Week 4		
Week 5		
Week 6		

OVERCOME WEAKNESSES

Overcoming our weaknesses is much less daunting than trying to turn them into strengths. When I (Analyn) embraced this truth, my life, time, energy, and potential opened up. This change also allowed me to embrace the strengths of others to help me be a better mom.

In chapter 9, we offered four strategies to overcome weaknesses. The strategies will help you guide a child to overcome weaknesses, but we want to use this portion of the Playbook to focus on you. The process calls us to humility and trust.

Managing Parenting Weaknesses

Take a look at your parenting strengths from the assessment in chapter 7 and consider some areas where you do not feel strong as a parent. Perhaps you will remember a few of the indicators in the assessment that did not resonate with you at all. Remember, the Five E's will not be evident in a weakness, and a weakness does not make you feel strong. With this in mind, pause for a few minutes and make a list of your parenting non-strengths/weaknesses in your journal. Now, lets consider the four strategies for overcoming weaknesses.

1. *Stop it.* If you are not strong at an activity, and it is not necessary for you to continue the activity, stop.

2. *Sub it out.* Consider which aspects of your parenting you can sub out in order to focus on your areas of strength.

3. *Sync up.* Partner with someone else who can help you overcome any areas of weakness.

4. *Support.* Overcome your weaknesses using tools and technology or service providers.

Look at your list of parenting non-strengths/weaknesses in your journal. Beside each item, write the number of the strategy you can use to help you overcome this area. Starting with just five non-strengths will help you make progress without becoming overwhelmed. Once you have the idea of how to utilize these strategies, you can pull from just about any of the non-strengths and engage one of the overcoming weakness strategies.

For each non-strength where you selected strategy 2 (sub it out), 3 (sync up), or 4 (support), consider your options for who or what you could look to for help. Your spouse is your first line of defense, and then comes your immediate family. Trusted friends and your church family are excellent resources. Don't forget professional service providers as well. We encourage you to spend time with this exercise and brainstorm in your journal.

FOCUS ON THE POSITIVE

The words we say are often written on the memories of our children. Our tone of voice, facial expression, and body language are also broadcasting our message. Therefore, as we wrote in chapter 10, it's important to filter our thoughts through God's Word and reframe our contemplations before they make their way out of our mouths and into the ears, minds, and hearts of our kids. We've learned there are many ways to communicate a positive message to our kids.

The Philippians 4:8 Filter

"Finally, brothers and sisters, whatever is true, whatever is noble, whatever is right, whatever is pure, whatever is lovely, whatever is admirable—if anything is excellent or praiseworthy—think about such things."

Now, using the Philippians 4:8 filter, think about your kids and note in your journal these eight positive descriptions of each child:

1. What is true about my child?
2. What is noble about my child?
3. What is right with my child?
4. What is pure about my child?
5. What is lovely about my child?
6. What is admirable about my child?
7. What is excellent about my child?
8. What is praiseworthy about my child?

The key to the Philippians 4:8 filter is to keep your comments positive! The Philippians 4:8 filter may be very natural for you, and you will find this exercise in line with how you already think about and speak to your child. On the other hand, this filter may take extra work. Stay the course. You are the primary voice of influence in the lives of your kids, especially when they are in their formative years.

Post a copy of your list somewhere you'll see it and be reminded to think of your child through the filter of God's Word.

Daily Scorecard: Keeping the 5:1 Ratio

Next, let's keep score of the interactions you have with your child for one day. Choose one child at a time and score the interactions you have with them or watch them have in the course of a day. You could make a chart like this in your journal:

Scorecard for _____ Date _____

Positive Interactions	Score	Negative Interactions	Score
Total Score:		Total Score:	

Total ratio of positive-to-negative interactions: _____

Try keeping score once a week for each of your kids. See if the meaningful scorecard helps you be mindful of staying positive even as you manage your own emotions and challenges throughout the day. As you progress, involve your kids in the process. Help them understand the importance of positive-to-negative interactions and the impact it could have on your entire family.

Discipline: From Punitive to Positive Reinforcement

Discipline is not something any of us look forward to, but it's necessary and vital to our children's development. With your Philippians 4:8 filter in place and giving mindful attention to the scorecard, we want to share with you another option when it comes to discipline: the Positive Sandwich.

To a child, discipline with love and acceptance feels different from discipline with anger or frustration. The Positive Sandwich has helped us immensely. Here is how it works: When you have an instructional conversation with your child, start with something positive about them. For example, you could recognize a well-meaning intent behind something they did. Next, offer the correction regarding their behavior. Be very clear: "This is what you did or said or didn't do, this is why I'm speaking to you about this, and this is the consequence." Then end on a positive: "Despite what you did, said, or didn't do, this is how I see you" (refer to the Philippines 4:8 filter).

The Positive Sandwich

Begin by pointing out something positive in your child.
Address the behavior that requires correction. Be clear as to the offense. Provide an example of the expected behavior and why it is important. Make the consequence meaningful and a point of learning.
End by identifying another positive trait in your child.

As we move from punitive to positive discipline, our kids feel the difference and learn to receive our reinforcement of their praiseworthy attributes. As a result, we can begin to learn specific ways to offer them praise in a way they will respond to.

Here's one last activity: Ask each of your kids what makes praise meaningful for them. Use the questions below and record their responses in your journal. This can become a priceless tool in your growth as a positive parent.

Meaningful Praise from My Child's Perspective

1. How do you like to be recognized when you do something great?

2. How often do you like to receive positive words from Mommy and Daddy?

3. What is your favorite way to be rewarded for a job well done?

4. How could Mommy and Daddy do a better job of making you feel important?

DECLARE THE TRUTH
OVER YOUR CHILDREN

We want to continually send our children the message that they matter to us because they matter to God. Your child is a gift, and you are an extension of their heavenly Father's love for them, so you'll want to take every opportunity to declare the truth of what you see and believe over your child.

Start with Scripture

When you stand on the truths of Scripture, you have the strength of the Lord as you parent your child. In chapter 11, we offer a list of Scripture passages to pray over your children and speak to them. When we mention declaring the truth over them, we simply mean speaking the words directly to them—or speaking the words about them when they're not with you. To get started, choose at least three of the Bible passages from the chapter (or ones you choose on your own), then write them on sticky notes and place them at strategic points in your home where you will see them frequently. Each time you see one of those posted verses, declare the truth of that passage over your child.

Do I Have What It Takes?

Each time your child faces a new challenge, they wonder whether they have what it takes. Every time your child faces peer pressure to go against their moral code, they will wonder, "Do I have what it takes to stand up when the going gets tough or the path is lonely?" Our job is to remind our kids over and over that they do, in fact, have what it takes to live a life from their strengths and their faith.

Take some time to jot down a few notes about each of your kids—what are they facing right now that might make them long to hear the words "You have what it takes"? After identifying a few items for each of them, commit to declare the truth over them until both you and they truly believe they do, in fact, have what it takes to overcome their next challenge.

Words to Live By

When your child is immersed in God's Word, they are more likely to understand how to live from their strengths to fulfill the calling God has placed on their life. This next exercise could very well lead to a lifelong tradition for your family and for each child. In fact, it might be one of the most simple and powerful activities you practice with your family.

Devote an hour or more to spend with your family and a Bible concordance or the word-search feature of your favorite online Bible resource. When you gather, present the assignment:

1. Together we will choose a family verse for the year. Everyone gets a say, a vote.

2. Then we'll decide how to display this verse in our home. Will it be on a chalkboard in the kitchen? Will we print, frame, and hang it in our entryway? Let the creative juices flow.

3. Next, each of us will choose a *personal* verse for the year.

4. Think of an empowering title for your verse, such as "My victory verse for the year," "My truth testament," or "My strength in the Lord Scripture."

It doesn't matter whether you start this in January or July. Decide how long this verse selection will be active and set a possible date for the next Bible verse brainstorm. Declaring your family's verse together and declaring your kids' personal verses in times of struggle and as daily encouragements can be tremendous gifts to your children!

SPOT STRENGTHS IN TODDLER TO TWEEN YEARS

Watching for signs of performance keeps us from projecting onto our young ones what we think they should do. Instead, we acknowledge areas of behavior that are distinct to the individual child. We'll explore a few ways to do this with little ones, and then we'll introduce some ways to notice and encourage the strengths in school-age kids, including tweens.

Toddlers at Play

Spotting strengths in your toddler can be as simple as observing them as they play. If you are deliberate about observing them and taking mental notes, you'll learn a lot. Set up a little one at a table with a set of crayons and a piece of paper. Do they lose themselves in the activity of making picture after picture? Are they quick to show you their creations and receive your encouragement or praise? Take notice of what they draw and ask them what they are creating.

Then choose a time to give them building blocks to play with. Do they get focused on building and creating this way? Will they spend lots of time on one creation or build, knock something down, and move on? Do they look to you to start the foundation for them to add to?

1. Watch for signs of performance. Where does your toddler exhibit above-average ability (making friends, playing with balls, following directions, thinking and then doing, playing with puzzles, verbally processing...)?

2. Look for places where your little one derives energy (playing in groups, being alone, reading books, doing arts and crafts…). They will be drawn to these activities and want to spend their time there. What are you noticing so far?

3. Observe if they prefer time with others or alone. For example, our Daniel has always enjoyed being with others as he played. The larger the group, the better! And David likes to work and play alone. If he adds one playmate, he's perfectly happy. What about your young one?

Looking for Strengths in School-Age Kids

You will really appreciate this suggestion to spot strengths: Assign chores! In our home, each of our children is assigned different weekly chores. Some of our kids really enjoy certain chores much more than others. When one of our kids takes to a certain chore, we're able to further develop their experience to truly master the chore.

For example, our daughter Madeline really enjoys preparing meals. She delights in cooking and baking, so we give her plenty of time to do this. Because Madeline enjoys this chore and has excelled in preparing different dishes, she has mastered preparing certain meals. We took this chore to the next level by having her create a menu for the week, check to see what we had in our pantry, and write a shopping list for the week.

Make a list of chores you commonly have your children do or reference the list below. Which chores is your child drawn to or most willing to help with most often? Which chores do they do well? How might they master their favorite chore categories?

If chores are not a big part of your family life, we encourage you to start. It is a way for the family to work together toward common goals and for you to live in discovery mode. It is a win-win for sure. Use the items below to help you create your own list of chores that would fit in your family's routine. Place your child's initials next to chores that they have done well or are drawn to, or initial those that could be good ones to introduce to them.

Chore List

feed and water animals	clean garage
garden	mop floors
vacuum	do laundry
dust	clean refrigerator
organize cabinets	clean pantry
remove clutter in living areas	organize toys
clean bathrooms	organize cabinets and drawers
collect garbage	
wash dishes	change bedding
prepare meals	wash windows
prepare sack lunches	weed flower beds
wash vehicles	touch up paint
mow the lawn	clean bedroom

Develop a Tween's Strengths

Help identify and develop a tween's strengths by practicing the active Three E's of strength development: engage, experiment, encourage. (These will help you through the teen years too.) This simple practice will help your child understand and develop their strengths. To help you apply these, we'll walk through an example of each using video game playing as an example.

Engage

David and Daniel earned a video game system as a reward for completing a series of assignments and performing well in their extracurricular activities. We noticed both boys really enjoyed a certain game, so we asked them why this game was so interesting. Turns out, they enjoyed playing with other friends online. We also learned Lance, Jordan, and Adam all played the same game.

Experiment

One family night, we invited David and Daniel to set up their video game system on the family television in our living room. We asked them to show us how to play their favorite game. We observed their different strategies and tactics. Their sister took a turn, and I (Brandon) eventually joined in as well. We were able to form a bond around their gaming through this participation experiment.

Encouragement

Watching the boys play and teach about their video game helped us see their *who* and not just their *do*. David and Daniel used very different strategies. Daniel was more aggressive and chose to go right to the action of the game; David was more conservative and chose to carefully consider each move. This observation gave us insights into their approaches to other activities and enabled us to praise each of them in their own unique way.

Practice the Three E's

Consider an activity that allows you to practice the Three E's. Write down your observations in your journal.

1. *Engage*—what activity can I use to engage my child? What are some questions I could ask?

2. *Experiment*—how could I experiment to learn more about my child?

3. *Encouragement*—what observation during the experiment can I use to encourage my child?

TRAIN TEENS AND
EMPOWER YOUNG ADULTS

Today we enjoy a wonderful relationship with our oldest daughter, Bailee. But during her teen and early young adult years, we could tell there was a breach in our relationship, and I (Brandon) knew I was responsible for this breach. As I evaluated my parenting approach during her teen years, I had to ask myself some key questions:

1. Did my parenting approach lead to my daughter's eyes shining?
2. Is my daughter confident in her strengths?
3. Do we have the type of relationship we both find fulfilling?
4. What could I do to bring restoration to our relationship?

I had long answers to each, but my short answer to the first three was "Not what I would have hoped for." This led me to question number 4. What could I do to bring about restoration? In a word, I could *engage* with my daughter.

For me, this first included an acknowledgment of my wrongs followed by an apology. In fact, I apologized more than once as I remembered key interactions that did not go well. After this, we took an interest in what my daughter was going through and found a way to be supportive. Over time, we experienced a shift—slowly, because true restoration takes time—and we are in a very healthy place today.

To deepen your relationship and perhaps bring some healing,

take some time to answer the four questions I considered. Watch out for defensiveness, because it surely will come. If you look past this initial rush of emotion, you will get to the heart of your opportunity.

Training Your Teen

In this chapter, our message to parents is to partner with your teen rather than have an adversarial role in their life. Below is an acrostic for the word "engage." Consider each word and note in your journal ways you can actively put these items into practice. We have provided examples and insights to help you stay in discovery mode.

Encourage your teens to serve others.

Example: I will take my son to coffee on Saturday morning to discuss the ways he enjoys serving others. I will encourage him in his God-given strengths to love people as Christ has loved him. I'll look for specific ways to help and will pray for him.

Negotiate with openness and active listening.

Teaching your teen to communicate and work through differing opinions is a life skill you can't just talk about; you have to model it. Establishing healthy dialogue during the teen years will serve you both well later. Practice asking what they feel is fair and why. Speak back to them what they state to you. Tell your child you appreciate their communication and respect their opinion.

Guide them through tough decisions.

Make a list of questions in your journal to ask your teen before giving your opinion. Questions should help them discover the answer on their own.

1. What are you leaning toward?
2. Which direction do you see yourself going more naturally?

3. Which direction brings you more joy?

4. What item will take you on the path that prepares you for your future?

Allow open communication without judgment.

Every day, encourage conversation with your teen. Sometimes they might say a swear word, make a statement you disagree with, or express a religious view that differs from yours. It's important to let them talk. Ask questions before injecting your thoughts, and sometimes, rather than correcting them, take it to prayer and have a follow-up conversation. This will require self-control and patience as you practice daily.

Gather their friends.

Partner with your teen to create opportunities for you to watch your teen interact with their friends. Consider hosting a game night or a postdance or postgame gathering. Invite friends to a family dinner, chaperone a teen trip, invite kids for a movie night, host a Bible study at a coffee shop, or host celebrations during the holidays.

Embrace them through failure.

When your teen confides in you or apologizes, you'll probably need to bite your tongue and swallow your pride. Resist the temptation to say "I told you so." Rather, express your gratitude for their honesty and offer your prayers and support.

Empowering Young Adults

Whether you are preparing to launch a young adult or are well into this stage, and regardless of how this process is going, remember this: *You can improve the relationship right where you're at.*

All of us desire to have close friendships with our adult children. However, to see this come to fruition, we must no longer see them as our kids and start seeing them as adults. You may wonder how to do that practically. Let's get started! Ask yourself these questions:

1. Does my adult son/daughter honestly, willingly share about personal struggles, hardships, or decisions? What can I do to open lines of communication with them?

2. Do I have clear boundaries with my adult son/daughter? How can I be sure to set clear boundaries and respect their autonomy?

3. Do I ever manipulate my adult son/daughter by expressing displeasure if they do not comply with my invitations or expectations? If so, how can I make sure to send invitations with an open hand and put my expectations in check?

4. Do I share my opinions freely without being asked by my adult son/daughter? How might I hold back from sharing unless asked to do so and with permission?

5. Do I actively pray for my adult son/daughter to have wisdom, favor, protection, and so on? Do I let them know I pray for them? Do I ask how to pray for them without invading their privacy? How could I more faithfully hold them in regular prayer?

6. Do I remain fascinated with my adult son/daughter? Do I ask questions and encourage their growth into adulthood? How could I do this more often?

Once you have considered these questions personally, ask your adult child their thoughts. Remember, the goal of these conversations is to grow your relationship with your adult son/daughter. It isn't a time to argue a perspective or remind them of an action you did in the past. Actively listen and speak their answers back to them to make sure you're understanding them. Make notes in your journal.

Support Your Young Adults' Strengths

At this stage in their development, their strengths should be apparent. However, it's helpful to check in to see how they are personally owning their strengths and utilizing them in their academic or professional endeavors. We enjoy asking each of our adult sons and daughters about their schooling, work life, and relationships to see if there's an opening to help them build up and use their strengths.

For example, early in our son-in-law Adam's career, he was faced with a work transition that would test his knowledge and expertise. When we discussed his new role, I (Brandon) was able to remind him of the strengths he possesses and how he could leverage these to be successful. Having the strengths of our young adults in mind allows us to always be ready when an opening appears to support them.

In your journal, make the following lists to stay aware of your adult child's strengths and success and what they have to teach you:

- ten strengths you see in your young adult
- ten times when you've seen those strengths in use
- ten successes your young adult has attained
- ten strengths they have used to attain success
- ten lessons you've learned from your young adult
- ten ways you've applied those lessons in your life

Don't forget to acknowledge what you have learned from your young adult and check in to see what they are learning. This way, you get to enjoy the growth process with them and increase your bond of friendship around common topics of interest.

Notes

Chapter 1: Inspire Your Kids to Shine

Epigraph: Cited in Kim Bongiorno, "40 Best Parenting Quotes of All Time," *Momtastic* (blog), http://www.momtastic.com/parenting/541137-40-amazing-quotes-parenthood/.

1. Benjamin Zander, "The Transformative Power of Classical Music," TED, February 2008, https://www.ted.com/talks/benjamin_zander_on_music_and_passion/transcript.

2. Zander, "The Transformative Power of Classical Music."

Chapter 2: Exchange Frustration for Fascination

1. L.R. Knost, *The Gentle Parent: Positive, Practical, Effective Discipline* (Little Hearts Books, 2013), 15.

2. Knost, *The Gentle Parent*, 55.

Chapter 3: Live in Discovery Mode

Epigraph: Mary Reckmeyer, *Strengths Based Parenting: Developing Your Children's Innate Talents* (New York: Gallup, 2016), 53.

1. Simon Sinek, *Start with Why* (New York: Portfolio, 2009), 42.

2. Sinek, *Start with Why*, 7.

3. Sinek, *Start with Why*, 50.

4. Donald O. Clifton and Paula Nelson, *Soar with Your Strengths* (New York: Dell, 1992), 20.

5. Marcus Buckingham and Donald O. Clifton, *Now, Discover Your Strengths* (New York: Free Press, 2001), 12.

6. Bronnie Ware, *The Top Five Regrets of the Dying* (Carlsbad, CA: Hay House, 2012), 37.

7. Reckmeyer, *Strengths Based Parenting*, 2.

Chapter 4: Identify and Honor Their Strengths

1. Jim Clifton, "Build Your Career Around Your Strengths, Not Your Weaknesses," *Chairman's Blog*, Gallup, February 2013, https://news.gallup.com/opinion/chairman/169277/build-career-around-strengths-not-weaknesses.aspx.

2. Michael Dauphinee, *Extraordinary* (Savage, MN: Broadstreet, 2018), 70.

Chapter 5: Uncover Their Calling

1. Cynthia McFadden and Jake Whitman, "Sheryl Sandberg Launches 'Ban Bossy' Campaign to Empower Girls to Lead," ABC News, March 10, 2014, https://abcnews.go.com/US/sheryl-sandberg-launches-ban-bossy-campaign-empower-girls/story?id=22819181.

2. John C. Maxwell, *The Leadership Handbook: 26 Critical Lessons Every Leader Needs* (Nashville: Thomas Nelson, 2008), 4.

3. Maxwell, *The Leadership Handbook*, 38.

4. Winston Churchill, special convocation, University of Miami, February 26, 1946.

Chapter 6: Activate the Ripple Effect

Epigraph: Scott Hagan, *The Language of Influence* (CreateSpace, 2016), 182.

1. Brent O'Bannon, *Let's Talk Strengths* (Sherman, TX: Strengths Champion, 2018), 23.

2. O'Bannon, *Let's Talk Strengths*, 23.

3. Maureen Electa Monte, *Destination Unstoppable: The Journey of No Teammate Left Behind* (Berkley, MI: Maureen Monte Consulting, 2016), 45.

Chapter 7: Seek *Your* Super

Epigraph: Edward "Chip" Anderson, "What Is Strengths-Based Education?" (PhD diss., Azusa Pacific University, 2004), 5.

1. Jim Clifton, "Build Your Career Around Your Strengths, Not Your Weaknesses," *Chairman's Blog*, Gallup, February 2013, https://news.gallup.com/opinion/chairman/169277/build-career-around -strengths-not-weaknesses.aspx.

2. Pauline Rose Clance and Suzanne Imes, "The Imposter Phenomenon in High Achieving Women: Dynamics and Therapeutic Intervention," *Psychotherapy Theory, Research and Practice* 15, no. 3 (1978).

3. Jordan Rosenfeld, "What Is Imposter Syndrome, and What Can You Do About It?," *Mental Floss*, February 20, 2016, http://mentalfloss.com/article/75699/what-imposter-syndrome -and-what-can-you-do-about-it.

4. Cited in Hyder Zahed, "Creating Fond Memories with Our Children," *HuffPost*, September 15, 2014, https://www.huffingtonpost.com/dr-hyder-zahed/creating-fond-memories-wi_b_5819982 .html.

Chapter 8: Don't Buy the Lies

Epigraph: Tom Rath, *Are You Fully Charged? The 3 Keys to Energizing Your Work and Life* (San Francisco: Silicon Guild, 2015), 55.

1. Rath, *Are You Fully Charged?*, 40.

2. Rath, *Are You Fully Charged?*, 40.

3. Tom Rath, *StrengthsFinder 2.0* (Washington, DC: Gallup, 2007), 20.

4. Marcus Buckingham, *Go Put Your Strengths to Work: 6 Powerful Steps to Achieve Outstanding Performance* (New York: Free Press, 2007), 85.

Chapter 9: Overcome Weaknesses

1. Donald O. Clifton and Paula Nelson, *Soar with Your Strengths* (New York: Dell, 1992), 19.

2. Nathan Giannini, "Daymond John Reveals How He Successfully Navigates His Dyslexia," AOL, October 31, 2015, https://www.aol.com/article/2015/10/31/daymond-john-reveals-how -he-successfully-navigates-his-dyslexia/21256726/.

3. Richard Feloni, "'Shark Tank' Investor Daymond John Explains How His Dyslexia Helped Shape Him into an Entrepreneur," *Business Insider*, December 6, 2015, https://www.businessinsider.com/ shark-tank-daymond-john-on-dyslexia-and-success-2015-12.

Chapter 10: Focus on the Positive

Epigraph: Stormie Omartian, *The Power of a Praying Parent* (Eugene, OR: Harvest House, 2014), 44.

1. Kyle Benson, "The Magic Relationship Ratio, According to Science," *Gottman Relationship Blog*, October 4, 2017, https://www.gottman.com/blog/the-magic-relationship-ratio-according-science/.

2. Donald O. Clifton and Paula Nelson, *Soar with Your Strengths* (New York: Dell, 1992), 31.

3. Lea Waters, *The Strength Switch: How the New Science of Strength-Based Parenting Can Help Your Child and Your Teen to Flourish* (New York: Avery, 2017), 249.

4. Timothy Davis, "The Power of Positive Parenting: Gottman's Magic Ratio," *Challenging Boys* (blog), October 21, 2010, http://challengingboys.com/the-power-of-positive-parenting-gottmans -magic-ratio.

5. Maureen Electa Monte, *Destination Unstoppable: The Journey of No Teammate Left Behind* (Berkley, MI: Maureen Monte Consulting, 2016), 166.

Chapter 11: Declare the Truth over Your Children

Epigraph: Luke 18:16.

1. John Eldredge, *Wild at Heart* (Nashville: Thomas Nelson, 2001), 5.

Chapter 12: Spot Strengths in Toddler to Tween Years

Epigraph: 3 John 4.

1. Mary Reckmeyer, *Strengths Based Parenting: Developing Your Children's Innate Talents* (New York: Gallup, 2016), 53.

2. Lea Waters, *The Strength Switch: How the New Science of Strength-Based Parenting Can Help Your Child and Your Teen to Flourish* (New York: Avery, 2017), 101.

3. Jennifer Fox, *Your Child's Strengths: Discover Them, Develop Them, Use Them* (New York: Viking, 2007), 98.

Chapter 13: Train Teens and Empower Young Adults

Epigraph: Paul David Tripp, *Age of Opportunity* (Phillipsburg, NJ: P&R, 1997), 192-93.

1. Jennifer Fox, *Your Child's Strengths: Discover Them, Develop Them, Use Them* (New York: Viking, 2007), 63.

2. Lea Waters, *The Strength Switch: How the New Science of Strength-Based Parenting Can Help Your Child and Your Teen to Flourish* (New York: Avery, 2017), 103.

3. Learn about this incredible young man at https://www.denisestimon.org, and learn more about We Dine Together at https://www.wedinetogether.org/about.

About the Authors

Analyn and Brandon Miller are successful business owners and the parents of seven children, spanning two generations. They are passionate about seeing families engage a strengths-based parenting approach that unearths the uniqueness in every child and empowers positive parent-child relationships through every stage of life.

Brandon is a certified strengths coach through the Gallup Organization and has been coaching and training strengths for more than 15 years. He is CEO of 34 Strong, an employee engagement and strengths-based development consultancy whose purpose is to build great places to work. Brandon is a former instructor at UC Davis and current professional speaker for Vistage International. Since the inception of 34 Strong, Brandon and his team have had the honor to work with Home Depot, Bank of America, Tesla, Johnson & Johnson, Hitachi, American Licorice Company, Genentech, Baptist Health, Johnson Controls, Plum Organics, Cascade Health, and GloryBee.

Analyn owns and operates the Analyn Miller Group, part of Keller Williams Realty. She holds the distinguished graduate real estate institute designation and is an outstanding life member of the Sacramento Masters Club. Together with her team, she takes great pride and pleasure in helping hundreds of families realize their dream of home ownership. As a full-time, hands-on mother, Analyn weaves together the priorities and strengths of the entire Miller family to facilitate a dynamic and intentional home culture.

Analyn and Brandon live in Elk Grove, California, and have served their local church in children, youth, and young-adult ministries. They have successfully launched their three adult children and are fully engaged in using the strengths approach to raise their four kids still at home. They also enjoy spending time with their first grandchild.

For additional free resources; to purchase support materials, including the Play Journal; or to contact Analyn and Brandon directly for speaking engagements, visit www.analynbrandon.com.

To learn more about Harvest House books and
to read sample chapters, visit our website:

www.harvesthousepublishers.com

HARVEST HOUSE PUBLISHERS
EUGENE, OREGON